THE STYLE BOOKLET

Fifth Edition, Revised

David Sonstroem
Department of English
University of Connecticut

McGraw-Hill Companies, Inc.
Primis Custom Publishing

New York St. Louis San Francisco Auckland Bogotá
Caracas Lisbon London Madrid Mexico Milan Montreal
New Delhi Paris San Juan Singapore Sydney Tokyo Toronto

McGraw·Hill

A Division of The McGraw·Hill Companies

THE STYLE BOOKLET

McGraw-Hill's Primis Custom Publishing consists of products that are produced from camera-ready copy. Peer review, class testing, and accuracy are primarily the responsibility of the author(s).

2 3 4 5 6 7 8 9 0 BKM BKM 9 0 9

ISBN 0-07-233832-6

Editor: Debbie Quigley
Cover Designer: Mark Anderson
Printer/Binder: Book-Mart Press, Inc.

Contents

Acknowledgments

The Style Booklet owes much to others. Foremost among my creditors is Alexander G. Medlicott, Jr., who spent many hours planning and improving the booklet and heartening me. I owe him special, cordial thanks. Over the years other members of the English Department have also contributed greatly in one way or another: John Abbott, Frederick Biggs, Rufus Blanshard, Lynn Z. Bloom, Bennett Brockman, Eric W. Carlson, Irving Cummings, A. Harris Fairbanks, John Gatta, Lee Jacobus, Thomas Jambeck, Veronica Makowsky, Matthew Proser, Compton Rees, Thomas J. Roberts, William Sheidley, Alexander Smith, Milton Stern, Janice Trecker, and Kenneth G. Wilson have kindly given useful advice or encouragement. Michael Meyer and J. D. O'Hara have not only given advice but also scrutinized earlier versions of the booklet in manuscript. Thomas Recchio has brought me up to date on bibliographical matters. The knowledgeable David A. Salomon has helped greatly in preparing the section on citing electronic sources. Evan Hill, former Head of the Journalism Department, Julius A. Elias, former Dean of the College of Liberal Arts and Sciences, and William L. Stull, Professor of English at the University of Hartford, have all made valuable suggestions. All have made the booklet better. The sole responsibility for remaining faults, both local and pervasive, rests with them.

Finally, this edition owes much to the enterprise of McGraw-Hill's Janie Pittendreigh, as well as to the advice, patience, and expertise of Lee M. Wolfe and Debbie Quigley, of McGraw-Hill, and Karen E. Fuller, of Architext.

The six lines of verse quoted in 4.5 are from "Gent," in Walker Gibson, *The Reckless Spenders*, Bloomington: Indiana UP, 1954, 44. Copyright 1954 by Indiana UP. The lines are quoted here with the permission of Indiana University Press.

To the Teacher

Several years ago the English Department at the University of Connecticut asked me to produce a pamphlet that would serve as a single, convenient source to which all its teachers could refer their students for advice on writing academic essays. The present *Style Booklet* is the repeatedly refined outcome of that request.

In the *Style Booklet* I set out to present as briefly as possible to the undergraduate essayist the main points of formal English composition. At first I expected to produce a twenty-page pamphlet, but as I proceeded, it lengthened. First, I encountered the comma, which stubbornly resisted cursory treatment. Second, I rediscovered the obvious: precepts are grasped more easily if accompanied by examples. And third, I decided that readableness was more important than brevity—that a bloodless fact sheet would seem far longer to the student reader than would half again as many pages of prose with a little life in them.

Although yielding on these points, I still resolved to be brief. For the sake of brevity I assumed the student's knowledge of elementary grammar as I set forth the conventions of formal English. I did, however, explain some of the more difficult grammatical concepts. Also for the sake of brevity I chose to treat formal English prescriptively rather than descriptively: instead of detailing all sides of an unsettled stylistic issue, I chose one correct alternative—usually a traditional one—and presented it with no ado. Most students, baffled or bored by unresolved stylistic alternatives, welcome a single, simple, correct solution to a stylistic problem. This booklet provides such directives.

In the booklet I try to instill my own belief that the little things of composition mean a lot—that a record of one's own ideas should be fussed over at least as lavishly as some piece of bric-a-brac that the student sanded and polished for hours back in Shop 121. I present the case for accuracy and care as strongly as I can, to urge the student to look at his or her composition with redoubled attention and solicitude. I believe that this is the appropriate place to speak pungently. I do so in good conscience, serene in the knowledge that you, the teacher, have the tact to soften the rigor for those—conscientious but ill prepared or overly nervous—who will learn more from tones more dulcet.

Whereas the typical handbook of grammar is too long to be read through with unglazed wits in less than a couple of weeks, this booklet can be read in a few hours. The teacher who assigns it can, therefore, confidently expect all students to be familiar with it. I believe it holds more information and good advice on style than any other work of like compass and hope it serves you and your students well.

To the Student

In this booklet the English Department presents some basic stylistic conventions, which it expects you to follow in all the standard academic essays you submit in its courses. The booklet treats such matters as how to arrange your essay on the page, how to punctuate, how to quote, and how to acknowledge secondary sources. It calls attention to the most frequently made stylistic faults of undergraduates' prose. And it offers some general advice on how to capture your best ideas in the web of language.

The booklet does not tell you how to arrange your ideas; that is your teacher's responsibility and, finally, yours. In addition, it does not tell you how to speak to your family or friends. The special language described (but not always used) here is called *formal English*: the language that professional, academic, literate people use while they are being strictly professional, academic, or literate. For the same reasons that you talk to your friends in their own way, you will want to write in the manner of an educated essayist when you are addressing educated readers of English. In short, the booklet asks you to develop one special kind of English but not as a substitute for the English you already know. Notice, though, that many of the points—those on punctuation, for instance—apply whether you are writing in the language of the learned journals or in the language of the streets.

The booklet does not replace a good, hardbound desk dictionary, such as *The American Heritage Dictionary*, *Merriam-Webster's Collegiate Dictionary*, or *The Random House Dictionary of the English Language*. Develop a meaningful relationship with one of these books. If you befriend it and keep it handy, it will serve you right. Always write an essay with your trusty dictionary at your side.

Nor does this booklet replace a handbook of grammar. You may need to consult such a handbook to review basic grammatical concepts. Although this booklet presents rules and conventions, it does not always pause to develop the terms in which they are given. A handbook of grammar does develop such terms.

The Style Booklet should serve, though, as a simple, compact reference work. Your teacher will assume your familiarity with the directives presented here or, at least, your ability to look them up when the occasion for applying them arises. Study the points carefully; refer to them thereafter whenever you are in doubt.

If you do not completely understand a point, turn to a handbook of grammar for a more extensive explanation of the terms in which point is given. If you still do not understand, ask your teacher for help. If the difficulties continue, you may need a course in basic English. If after consulting a handbook you cannot tell a phrase from a clause, a sentence from a fragment, the nominative case from the objective, or a gerund from a participle, take such a course. A good start is half the race.

If your curiosity about prose style goes beyond the brief treatment given it here, you may wish to browse in some of the books listed in the bibliography. You may also wish to consult these books if you need a more extensive account of how to cite works in a scholarly paper. For the latter purpose the fourth, 1995 edition of the *MLA Handbook for Writers of Research Papers* or the third, 1994 edition of Michael Meyer, *The Little, Brown Guide to Writing Research Papers* are especially useful. Both are available at most academic bookstores. See, too, the end of chapter 8 for a list of style manuals for academic fields outside the humanities.

Although plagiarism is not a grammatical or stylistic matter, it is sometimes a sad reality of academic life, so this booklet includes a chapter on it. You must read the chapter, for you will be held accountable for knowing what is in it. Learn exactly what plagiarism is; understand why it is forbidden; appreciate the severity of the penalty for it; avoid it.

Sentences composed to illustrate points of grammar tend to be dull and vacuous. To rouse this dormant genre, I have tried to make my illustrations appealing to the young at heart. As a result, the tone and diction of some of the illustrations are inappropriate to academic discourse. Sift the wheat from the chaffing: in your academic essays apply the points of grammar and style to a more decorous prose, suited to vigorous intellectual exposition. Your essays need not be stiff-rumped or solemn, but they should sound and be appropriately serious.

This booklet should help you shape and order your prose, thereby clearing your mind for more important, substantive considerations. Merely observing all the conventions treated in the booklet is, of course, not enough to make you a good writer, but it will certainly contribute.

Moreover, failing to observe them may well keep a reader from appreciating your best ideas or keep you from bringing your ideas to their best form. Writing precisely is part of thinking straight.

—David Sonstroem

1. Format

Write at least the last draft of your essay with a typewriter or computer. Type is far more readable than longhand and gives your essay a polished, professional look. Many teachers will not accept an essay submitted in longhand.

The typewritten paper

1.1.1   Write on only one side of a sheet. Choose typing paper of the standard size (8 1/2" x 11"). A good, plain bond paper is best, but if you find bond too costly, choose instead any plain white paper. But avoid very thin, "onionskin" paper. And avoid "corrasable" paper, which smudges easily and repels ink (most teachers would rather correct an essay written on Saran Wrap than one on erasable bond). If you are all thumbs and must type on erasable bond, submit a photocopy of the typed essay.

1.1.2   Number all pages consecutively. If you choose to have a title page, do not include it in your enumeration. Do include the first page of text in your enumeration but do not type its number. The title, centered at the top of page 1, suffices to mark the page as your first. Type your name (or last name) followed by the page-number on each page. Type them half an inch below the top of the sheet and one inch in from the right edge of the sheet.

1.1.3   Leave one-inch-wide margins at the top, bottom, and right side of the page. Leave one and one-quarter inches for the left margin, so that your teacher has room for extensive local comments.

1.1.4   Unless your teacher directs otherwise, give your essay a title, which specifies your main point. Do not put quotation marks around the title; do not underline it; do not put a period after it. Capitalize the first and last words of the title and the first word after a colon or semicolon. Capitalize, too, all other words except articles, prepositions, coordinating conjunctions, and the *to* of the infinitive. Leave an extra line between the title and the beginning of your text.

1.1.5   Double-space between your lines. Do not use space-and-one-half spacing, which is handsome but leaves too little room for your teacher's remarks. It is all right to ink in a few minor corrections, but if major corrections are necessary, retype the page. Indent five spaces at the start of each paragraph.

1.1.6   Single-space between words; double-space between sentences. Single-space after commas, colons, and semicolons.

1.1.7   Present legible, neat work. Use a black ribbon only—no red. Replace the ribbon immediately when it begins to fade. Keep the typeface of your keys clean (all stationers sell inexpensive products for this purpose). Catch typographical errors as you make them, erase thoroughly with a typing eraser or white overcoating substance, and retype your corrections. You may print a few corrections neatly in ink above mistakes, which are scored through with a single line. But type corrections whenever possible and, if the mistakes mount up, retype the page.

1.1.8   Use a paper clip, not a staple, to join the pages of your essay. A staple hinders your teacher from seeing more than one page of your essay at a time. For the same reason do not bind your essay within cardboard or plastic covers.

1.1.9   Keep a carbon or photocopy until the essay is returned to you.

1.2 | **The paper written with a computer**

Typing your paper on a computer is the best option. Clumsy typists are grateful for the ease with which corrections can be made. Papers produced on a computer are generally more presentable than those produced on a typewriter. You can use the powers of the computer to help you check spelling and grammar. And you can easily produce a copy of your essay if the original is lost.

But when writing an academic essay, resist showing off all the powers of your computer and all your desktop-publishing expertise. Teachers and editors like to work with plain, straightforward text that is easy to read and emend. They want your essay to show up not in its fanciest party clothes but in a hospital johnny, which allows for easy examination and, if need be, surgery. So if you use a computer, observe the following points:

1.2.1 Make your essay look similar to a typewritten one. To this end, follow the directives given for the typed paper. Choose a good, readable font, such as Times New Roman or Courier; do not change type styles in mid-essay; do not use boldface, except (if you wish) for the title or for divisions of the essay; underline to indicate italics; choose a ragged-right margin, not a right-justified margin. In addition, use a letter-quality or near-letter-quality printer. If a dot-matrix printer is the only kind available, use it in its most readable mode.

1.2.2 If your essay is printed on a continuous roll of paper, tear off the perforated strip from each side of the roll and separate the pages.

1.2.3 By all means, use your word processor's spelling checker. It finds many misspellings that even the careful proofreader misses. However, you will still have to proofread, because the program cannot find misspellings disguised as other, correctly spelled words. Only the human brain can distinguish among *to, too,* and *too*; *their, there,* and *they're*; *accept* and *except*; *here* and *hear*.

1.3   **The handwritten paper**

Unless you have a black belt in calligraphy, the handwritten paper does not do your work justice. Type instead. But if your teacher lets you submit a paper in longhand and if you absolutely must do so, read through all the rules for the typewritten paper and apply them as closely as you can to the handwritten paper. In addition, observe the following:

1.3.1   Use 8 ½ x 11" narrow-lined paper. Do not use sheets torn out of a notebook. Those fuzzy, square-toothed edges snag other papers and shed flakes of fibrous dandruff on your teacher's tweeds. Write on every other line of only one side of a sheet. Be especially careful to leave one-inch margins at the right and bottom of your page, in addition to the standard margins at the left and top. Choose a sober blue or black ink rather than an exotic pastel. Never submit an essay in pencil.

1.3.2   Because you do not type, you are obliged to outdo yourself in producing a neat, clear script. Some readers believe that sloppy handwriting is a sign of sloppy thinking. They may be wrong, but you will find it safer to avoid their prejudice than to try to disabuse them of it. If your printing is more legible than your cursive script, print.

1.3.3   Avoid a large, sprawling scrawl. Handwriting on every other line produces a page with fewer words than are contained on a typed page. The fewer words per page, the harder it is for you and your reader to discern your train of thought. So everyone will benefit if you master a fairly compact script. You must not, of course, sacrifice legibility to attain it.

2. Spelling

Careless spelling is the least forgivable sin of composition. Careless spelling, not incompetent spelling; lack of effort, not poor training or native inability. Many of us cannot remember the correct spelling of words. Our shortcoming is nothing to be ashamed of, just as we should not be ashamed if we are not tall, swift, or muscular. Teachers tend to overlook misspellings on tests, where students cannot make amends for this weakness.

But correct spelling in an essay assigned days before it is due consists of more than remembering. We can divide the spelling process into three distinct stages: (1) remembering the spelling of words, (2) looking up in a dictionary the spelling of words of which we are unsure, and (3) proofreading the final draft of the essay for mistakes in transcription. Fortunately, we bad spellers can compensate completely for our shortcoming by working hard at stages 2 and 3. Unfortunately, even spelling bee champions can betray their gift through carelessness at stages 2 and 3.

Although stages 2 and 3 require little talent, they do require considerable effort. The effort is worth expending. Shirking at these stages shows discourtesy to the reader as well as contempt for one's own ideas. A teacher may well undervalue ideas that students themselves treat carelessly. And the outside world is harsher still. One of life's many ironies is that although many students consider spelling an unimportant part of writing, the common reader often uses it as an important basis for judgment. Because of a single misspelling, many a letter to the editor and many a job application has been tossed into the wastebasket. To help you in your spelling, here are some suggestions for each stage of the process:

2.1   To save time, you will want to make the most of your ability to remember the spelling of words. To improve your spelling memory,

- Keep a notebook in which you write down words whose spelling you must look up. Memorize the spelling of them.

- Every time you turn to your dictionary to look up the spelling of a word, circle the word in pencil. The practice supplies you with a handy source of slippery words.

- Look up in your handbook of grammar a list of frequently misspelled words. Study them, a few at a time.

- Make a point of visualizing troublesome words. Some people find it easier to recall the image of a word than to learn its spelling by rote.

- Because mispronunciation often lies behind a misspelling, take pains to pronounce words properly.

- See your handbook of grammar for some guidelines to spelling, such as "*I* before *e* except after *c*." Such guidelines cover the spelling of most words, so knowing the guidelines will lengthen the life of your dictionary.

What works for one person may not work for another. Choose for yourself whatever practices help you most.

2.2   However well you spell, you will never be able to dispense with a dictionary. Here are some hints for this stage:

- Make looking up all words of whose spelling you are unsure an invariable habit. Do not sit down to write unless you have a dictionary at hand.

- The dictionary gives the potentially troublesome forms of a word in addition to the basic word itself. For example, your dictionary informs you that the plural of *hero* is formed *-roes* but the plural of *tyro* is *-ros*; it informs you that the past tense of *refer* is *-ferred* but the past tense of *differ* is *-fered*. Look up the basic word to learn the spelling of its several forms.

- You may wish to buy a spelling dictionary: a book that gives words in alphabetical order but without definitions. Because a spelling dictionary is more compact than a regular dictionary, it reduces the time spent in locating words.

- Beware of proper nouns: place names, authors' names, the names of characters in novels, the names of corporations, and the like. They are misspelled with dismaying frequency. A good desk dictionary includes proper nouns. Because some dictionaries give biographical or geographical names in a separate listing, you may have to consult the dictionary's table of contents to find the proper noun whose spelling you wish to verify.

- If you know you know the spelling of a word, all well and good; if you merely think you know its spelling, look it up. In so doing, you will certify its spelling and perhaps secure it in your mind once and for all.

2.3   Proofreading the final draft is much more difficult than one might suppose. Errors made in transcription are devilishly hard to spot. Writers are easily lured away from considering their words as mere objects to revel instead in the warm flow of their own ideas.

- If you are so tempted, read your lines word by word from right to left.

- If you are using a computer with a program that checks spelling, use the program. But because the program cannot mark words misspelled as other, correctly spelled words, you will still have to proofread the old-fashioned way, to distinguish among *to, too*, and *too*; *there, their*, and *they're*; *accept* and *except*; *here* and *hear*. A good program will, though, quickly identify many misspellings that might have escaped your notice.

- Take frequent breaks. Only fresh eyes can proofread.

- Once is not enough. Once is not enough.

3. Punctuation: The Comma

The commonest type of writing error is improper punctuation. Many people punctuate by Ouija Board or (what is much the same thing) by ear. Although the ear will sometimes lead one to the appropriate mark, the brain is a more reliable guide.

The following system of punctuation is as definite and clear-cut as I could make it. It leaves as little as possible to intuition and includes as few alternatives and exceptions as the living language allows. I present such a system for two reasons: First, it is far easier to learn than a system rubbery with options, exceptions, and exemptions. And second, it provides the basis for nuance. One cannot even depart meaningfully from the norm where no norm has been established. Before a string can vibrate, it must be taut.

I discuss the comma first because it is by far the most difficult mark to master. In fact, in learning the rules for using the comma, you will rehearse almost all you need to know about the structure of the English sentence. The next chapter discusses far more briefly in alphabetical order thirteen other marks: the apostrophe, brackets, the colon, the dash, the ellipsis, the exclamation point, the hyphen, parentheses, the period, the question mark, quotation marks, the semicolon, and the slash. You may have to look up some terms in your handbook to understand all the rules.

The comma is potentially a subtle instrument, yet often it is merely sprinkled into essays, like pepper onto poached eggs. A rough-and-ready account of the comma is that it marks pauses within a sentence. A more accurate account is that the comma *clarifies the structure of a sentence*. It does so in several ways.

3.1 | **Independent Clauses**

The comma plus one of seven connectives—*and, but, or, nor, for, so*, and *yet*—may be used to join main (independent) clauses.

What is a clause? A **clause** is a syntactically related word-group forming a segment of a sentence and containing a subject and predicate verb. Do not confuse a clause with a phrase: a **phrase**, too, is a syntactically related word-group, but it lacks a predicate verb. Because verbals do not serve as predicate verbs, verbals and their modifiers form phrases, not clauses, although all verbals are verb forms, and the infinitive can even have a subject. I shall return to phrases shortly. For now let us consider clauses.

Clauses are either dependent (subordinate) or independent (main). A **dependent** clause serves as a noun, adjective, or adverb in another clause. An **independent clause** does not: it is not absorbed into the syntax of another clause.

When a sentence consists of two (or more) independent clauses, the clauses may be joined by a comma plus one of seven connectives (called **coordinating conjunctions**):

$$
\text{main clause} + \text{comma} +
\begin{cases}
and \\
but \\
or \\
nor \\
for \\
so \\
yet
\end{cases}
+ \text{main clause}
$$

Virginia Creeper is overly cautious, **but** Penny Arcade treats life as one big game.

Be careful in applying this rule, for it is easily misunderstood. Avoid the pitfalls discussed in the three cautionary notes that follow:

3.1.1 Any of these connectives is used *without* a comma when what is paired is *not* two main clauses.

> She is playful **but** cautious.

The sentence consists of only one clause; *but* joins two adjectives. Hence *but* is not preceded by a comma.

3.1.2 All other connectives (for example, conjunctive adverbs, such as *hence, however,* and *therefore,* or conjunctive adverbial phrases, such as *in fact* and *on the other hand*) are preceded by a semicolon when they join main clauses. Compare

> I do not care who wins the election**, so** I shall not vote.

with

> I do not care who wins the election**; therefore**, I shall not vote.

In the latter example two main clauses are joined by *therefore* rather than by one of the above-mentioned seven connectives; therefore *therefore* is preceded by a semicolon.

3.1.3 Two main clauses may also be joined by a semicolon alone:

> Virginia is cautious; Penny treats life as a game.

Or they may be made into two simple sentences:

> Virginia is cautious. Penny treats life as a game.

We have, then, three alternatives for joining independent clauses:

- Comma plus coordinating conjunction

- Semicolon (plus a conjunctive adverb, if the meaning calls for it)

- Period (plus a conjunctive adverb, if the meaning calls for it)

Of course, a period turns the independent clauses into simple sentences. The choice among these three alternatives is a matter of rhetorical tactics rather than of grammar.

When two main clauses are joined in some way other than the three alternatives just mentioned—if they are joined, for instance, by just a comma or by no punctuation mark at all—the result is the grammatical error a **run-on sentence** (another term for main clauses joined by just a comma is **comma splice**). Because many readers consider comma splices and other run-on sentences a major lapse in literacy, it is to your advantage to know what main clauses are and how to join them.

3.2   Adjective Clauses, Phrases, and Nouns
Use commas to set off nonrestrictive clauses as well as nonrestrictive phrases and nouns. Use no punctuation to set off restrictive clauses, phrases, and nouns.

As was mentioned in 3.1, a dependent clause serves in another clause as a noun, adjective, or adverb. Punctuating noun clauses poses no difficulty, so I do not discuss them. I shall, however, treat adjective clauses and adverb clauses.

Adjective clauses—and, we may as well add at once, adjective phrases and nouns—are either restrictive or nonrestrictive. A **restrictive** clause, phrase, or noun is one that narrows the scope of a noun. It answers the question "Which one?" A **nonrestrictive** clause, phrase, or noun is one that modifies a noun without narrowing its scope. In the expression "girls who wear purple shoes," the clause "who wear purple shoes" limits girls (a very extensive group) to purple-shod girls (a much smaller group). On the other hand, in the expression "Mom, who sported purple pumps," the clause does not in the least reduce that group of one member, dear old Mom.

The comma helps the writer convey this distinction.

My brother, Billy, raises peanuts and Cain.

My brother_Billy_raises peanuts and Cain.

In the first example the commas framing "Billy" signify that what is contained within them is somewhat parenthetical: it enriches or embellishes the basic meaning of the sentence but does not establish it. The commas announce that "Billy" does not restrict "brother," so the reader infers that Billy is my only brother. Conversely, the absence of commas in the second sentence implies the existence of at least one more brother.

This rule is observed in the following sentences. Note the appropriateness of the commas or of the absence thereof:

He calls the athlete_who excels in many sports_a "jock of all trades."

He called on his aunt, who was not in a mood to see him.

The word_*polyphiloprogenitive*_is more easily pronounced than the word_*coupon*.

That single name, "E. F. Hutton," growled through clenched teeth and curled lips, rendered the whole room suddenly still.

3.3   Adverb Clauses

When any adverb clause precedes its main clause, it is followed by a comma. When a stressed adverb clause follows its main clause, it is not preceded by a comma; when an unstressed adverb clause follows its main clause, it is preceded by a comma.

3.3.1   An adverb, you will remember, modifies a verb, adjective, or other adverb. Adverb *clauses* seldom modify adjectives or adverbs, almost always modifying instead the predicate verb of another clause. An adverb clause is usually placed either before or after the clause whose predicate verb it modifies. When it precedes the clause, it is followed by a comma, which signals the transition from one clause to the next. There is no need for such a mark when the adverb clause follows the main clause: the opening word of the adverb clause (for example, *before, when, because, where, although*) is enough to announce that a new clause is underway.

Any adverb clause, main clause.

Main clause_stressed adverb clause.

When I am tired, I cannot sleep.

I cannot sleep_when I am tired.

When, however, a trailing adverb clause is not stressed—when it is less important to the point that the writer is making than the main clause—it is preceded by a comma, which reports the secondary, parenthetical nature of the trailing clause.

Whether an adverb clause is stressed or unstressed cannot always be deduced simply from the words of the sentence. Instead the writer asks whether the (almost always implicit) question being answered by the sentence is answered in the main clause or in the trailing adverb clause. If the question is answered in the main clause, then the trailing adverb clause is secondary, so it is preceded by a comma. If, though, the question is answered in the trailing adverb clause, then the adverb clause is stressed, so no comma precedes it. Appreciate the differences in nuance among the following paired sentences:

> I wash my hair with Oxydol_because I think I'm worth it.

> I wash my hair with Oxydol, because I think I'm worth it.

> Amazing Grace sang "On My Journey Home"_after the enthusiastic applause had abated.

> Amazing Grace sang "On My Journey Home," after the enthusiastic applause had abated.

The first sentence of each pair answers an implicit *adverbial* question, requiring the causal or temporal conjunction: *Why* do you wash your hair with Oxydol? *When* did Grace sing "On My Journey Home"? The second sentence of each pair answers an implicit question not requiring such a connective: What laundry product leaves your hair so lovely? What did Grace sing? Here each adverb clause supplies gratuitous information—a fact heralded by the comma preceding it.

3.3.2 All introductory **verbal phrases**, as well as adverbial verbal phrases appearing elsewhere in the sentence, are punctuated according to the rule for adverb clauses:

> To win World War II, first graders picked bags and bags of milkweed pods.

> You must open hundreds of oysters_to find a pearl.

3.4 | **Adverb Phrases**

Put a comma after an introductory adverb phrase of seven words or more. Do not put a comma (or any other punctuation) after an introductory adverb phrase of six words or fewer.

There are many kinds of phrases, but only a few kinds require special rules of punctuation. As has already been stated in 3.2, adjective phrases are punctuated according to the rule given for adjective clauses.

But the rule for adverb phrases is different from that for adverb clauses. Unlike introductory adverb clauses, introductory adverb phrases seldom disguise the syntax of the rest of the sentence. So the comma is seldom needed to mark the close of an introductory phrase. Compare

> Before Cliff Dweller died, no one had heard of him.

with

> After his death_no one heard of him either.

The first sentence is introduced by an adverb clause, which is followed by a comma; the second, by an adverb phrase, which is not followed by a comma.

The "rule of sixes and sevens" is easy to apply to introductory adverb phrases:

> Over the meadow and through the woods, to Grandmother's house we go.

> In the spring_a young man's fancy lightly continues to dwell on thoughts of love.

The first sentence is introduced by an adverb phrase of seven words, so the phrase is followed by a comma; the second sentence, by an adverb phrase of three words, so the phrase is not followed by a comma.

There are, however, three exceptions to Rule 3.4:

3.4.1 As we saw in Rule 3.3., introductory *verbal* phrases, no matter how brief, are always followed by a comma.

3.4.2 *Conventional* introductory words or phrases, such as *indeed, well, on the other hand, in fact, on the contrary, of course*, or *finally*, are followed by a comma. For example, compare these sentences:

> On the stage_Billy Doux was a terrific hit.

> On the other hand, Belle Bottom was a terrible flop.

In sentences where there is no pause after a conventional introductory term, the comma is optional:

> In fact, he was born laughing.

> In fact_he was born laughing.

3.4.3 Rule 3.9, given below, can override Rule 3.4.

3.5 **Terms in Series**
Use commas to separate all terms of a series from one another.

Journalists as well as American Anglophiles omit the comma before the final member of a series (e.g., "war, pestilence_and famine"), but phonetics, semantics, and American convention all argue for a comma there. One argument: a comma so placed allows more syntactic variety than is available without it.

The terms of a series may be single words, phrases of all kinds, and—in rare instances—clauses.

> His favorite cities are Sandusky, Bridgeport, and Chattanooga.
>
> *[nouns]*

> She longed to go to the shore, the mountains, to the moon.
>
> *[prepositional phrases]*

He arose, showered, dressed, ate his Cheerios, and spent the day in his room, questioning the meaning of life.

[predicates]

Section 3.1 presents various ways to punctuate joined independent clauses. None of the ways consists of just a comma. I am about to discuss an optional exception. When independent clauses are *brief and syntactically parallel*, they may be joined by a comma alone. And even then the comma is a rarity. When you do use a comma in this situation, it conveys an impression of rush and excitement. The first of the following sentences suggests stolid deliberation or inevitability; the second, suddenness and exultation:

I came; I saw; I conquered.

I came, I saw, I conquered.

Choose the punctuation that enhances the mood you wish to convey.

Adjectives in series present a special problem. Like most other coordinate terms, *coordinate* adjectives are separated by commas:

Before that withered, frail, sickly man took up weightlifting, he looked like Arnold Schwarzenegger in his prime.

But adjectives may also be arranged in a *hierarchical* series, the terms of which are *not* separated by commas:

That dear_little_old man is a convicted murderer.

In the first example all the adjectives modify equally the noun that follows them. In the second example each adjective modifies all that comes after it in the phrase, some adjectives thus modifying more words than do other adjectives:

old, frail, sickly man

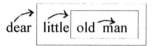

dear | little | old man

If you have difficulty making this distinction, practice with specific sentences. To distinguish, remember that those adjectives that could tolerate rearrangement or the placement of *and* between them are coordinate; those that could not are hierarchical.

3.6 Parenthetical Terms

Use the comma to segregate a parenthetical word, phrase, or clause from the rest of the sentence or major clause. If the parenthetical term comes at the beginning or end of the sentence, you will need one comma; if it comes in the middle, two.

Note that Sections 3.2, 3.3, and 3.4 may be seen as specifically directed applications of this rule.

> To be sure, college is never the best place for the really serious student.

> I am, of course, a genius.

> I do not like thee, Doctor Fell.

If commas do not bury an interjected term as much as you would like, use parentheses instead. If commas do not call attention to the interjected term as much as you would like, use dashes instead. Note in the following three sentences the increasing prominence given the interjected term, together with the decreasing prominence given the basic sentence, which frames it:

> April showers (Martha declared solemnly) may bring flowers.

> April showers, Martha declared solemnly, may bring flowers.

April showers—Martha declared solemnly—may bring flowers.

In addition, parentheses can imply confidentiality; dashes, spontaneity of utterance. More often than not, commas are the best choice.

3.7 Other Uses of the Comma

See 4.11.1 for using the comma to punctuate direct discourse. See chapters 7, 8, and 9 for using the comma to punctuate notes and bibliographies.

The following examples show the use of the comma in giving addresses, dates, and geographical names:

George N. Fenn, DMD, was my dentist.

Mr. Frederick Bloominstock, Jr., of Columbus, Indiana, announced that June 25, 2007, would be doomsday. [*or* . . . 25 June 2007 would be doomsday.]

Bristol, Conn._06010

3.8 Improper Commas

Unless a construction that takes commas comes between subject and predicate verb, do not put a comma between subject and predicate verb. Unless a construction that takes commas comes between predicate verb and the verb's direct object or other complement(s), do not put a comma between predicate verb and the verb's direct object or other complement(s).

The previously presented rules for using the comma are quite enough. None prescribes a comma between subject and predicate verb or between predicate verb and its object. A comma in either of these positions sends a false syntactic signal.

Wrong: Little Jack Horner, sat in the corner.

Wrong: Mary had, a little lamb.

But commas are, of course, appropriate when intervening constructions, often parenthetical, call for them:

Appropriate: Little Jack Horner, late as usual for brunch, sat in the corner.

Appropriate: Mary had, much to the chagrin of her control-freak teacher, a little lamb.

3.9   Irregular Commas

Now and then you will find it necessary to insert an irregular comma to prevent confusion. Making sense takes priority over marking syntactic structure.

Outside, the rhododendrons sported huge, gaudy blossoms.

Out of the blue, washday miracles began to occur.

According to rule 3.4, there should be no comma after "Outside" or "Out of the blue." But deprived of the commas, the reader would mistakenly proceed, "Outside the rhododendrons . . ." and "Out of the blue washday. . . ."

4. Punctuation: The Other Marks

The comma is discussed in chapter 3. The other marks are discussed here in alphabetical order.

The Apostrophe

The apostrophe is threatened with extinction. One teacher predicts that the apostrophe will disappear altogether, except for the possessive pronoun *it's* (where the mark is a trespasser). Despite ostracism and abuse, the apostrophe remains an informative mark when used properly.

4.1.1 Excepting the pronouns *my, your(s), his, her(s), its, our(s), their(s)*, and *whose*, use the apostrophe to indicate the possessive case of nouns and pronouns. To form the possessive of singular nouns, add **'s**. To form the possessive of plural nouns ending in **s**, add merely the apostrophe. To form the possessive of plural nouns not ending **s**, add **'s**.

> a lady's room
>
> the ladies' room
>
> women's rights

Four notes to this rule may help:

4.1.1.1 All pronouns except those listed in 4.1.1 do take the apostrophe: *one's* dignity, *somebody's* mother, *others'* feelings.

4.1.12   Grammarians disagree over whether to add an *s* after the apostrophe in giving the possessive of singular nouns ending in *s*. Should one write "for goodness' sake" or "for goodness's sake"? "The Prince of Wales' sore thumb" or "The Prince of Wales's sore thumb"? Until grammarians do agree, take the easiest road: treat these singular nouns exactly as you do all others, namely, always add **'s**.

4.1.13   In dealing with pairs, show individual possession by adding the appropriate possessive ending to each term; show joint possession by adding the ending to the latter term only.

Donnie's and Marie's relentless smiles

Donnie and Marie's closing number

4.1.1.4   To form the possessive of a compound noun or noun phrase, add the appropriate ending to the last word only.

Franklin Delano Roosevelt, Jr.'s marriage

Alfred, Lord Tennyson's poetry

Everyone else's troubles

the three ladies-in-waiting's gowns

4.1.2   Use the apostrophe to signify omitted letters in standard contractions: *don't, wouldn't, they're*. But note that although contractions are quite acceptable in everyday conversation, they are rarely used in formal writing.

4.1.3 Use the apostrophe and **s** to form the plural of letters, symbols, and words referred to as words. However, do not use the apostrophe—add just the *s*—to form the plural of numerals and abbreviations.

Minding your *p*'s and *q*'s is not so easy as *abc*.

All his *garbage's* rhyme with his *cabbage's*.

but

How many PhDs did Yale produce in the 1960s?

4.2 | **Brackets**

Squared parentheses, called brackets, serve two limited but useful functions:

4.2.1 Brackets distinguish a writer's interjected additions from quoted matter:

Oscar Wilde remarked, "[George] Meredith is a prose [Robert] Browning, and so is Browning."

One unconscious Aesop wrote, "We must avoid all chickanery [sic] and hippocrisy [sic]."

4.2.2 Brackets indicate a parenthesis within a parenthesis. But, for the sake of clarity, avoid this involved construction if you can.

The DEP (Department of Environmental Protection [or, as one critic would have it, Does Everything Poorly]) is in bad need of protection itself these days.

If your typewriter does not have brackets, skip the appropriate spaces and then ink in brackets by hand.

According to *Annals of the South*, "Jimson Weed ⌈well-known ante bellum tobacco grower and corrupt legislator⌉ dropped from sight forever on the evening of 31 February 1859."

4.3 | The Colon

The colon promises an immediate resolution. It points ahead, announcing that the expectation created by the part of the sentence preceding it is about to be satisfied. It declares that the awaited example, definition, summary, or answer is at hand. It might be translated, "that is," "namely," or "in sum." Often it is accompanied by a reinforcing expression, such as *as follows*. Furthermore, when used in complete sentences, the colon follows a complete syntactic construction. In other words, what the colon announces should not serve as direct object or subject complement of its clause or verbal phrase or as object of a preposition.

> **Wrong**:   Today I learned to spell: *embarrass*, *accommodate*, and *definitely*.

> **Right**:   Today I learned to spell three words: *embarrass*, *accommodate*, and *definitely*.

> **Wrong**:   Emerging from the wilderness after twenty-one days, he wondered only: how are the Red Sox doing?

> **Right**:   Emerging from the wilderness after twenty-one days, he had only one thought on his mind: how are the Red Sox doing?

In the first example, what follows the colon serves wrongly as direct object of the infinitive; in the third, what follows the colon serves wrongly as direct object of the clause.

Unless the colon introduces an indented quotation, do not capitalize after a colon, even if what follows could stand as a complete sentence. Of course, if the first word after the colon is capitalized in its own right (for example, a proper noun or the first word of a quoted sentence), it retains its capital. Also, if the colon announces a list of sentences introduced by numbers ("Second ... Third. . ."), then, for the sake of uniformity, capitalize "First."

The colon does a few odd jobs on the side. It follows the salutation of a business letter. It separates numerals in biblical and temporal notation. It separates titles from subtitles. And as we shall see in chapters 8 and 9, it serves some other bibliographical functions.

Dear President Austin:

Genesis 1:20

4:27 A.M.

Vanity Fair: A Novel without a Hero

Willimantic, CT: Curbstone Press

The modern practice is to skip a *single* space after the colon. But note the exceptions in the examples just preceding.

4.4 | **The Dash**

Typed, the dash consists of two unspaced hyphens--thus. Most computer programs include a one-em dash—thus. In either form, the dash takes no spaces immediately before or after it. Use the dash to mark the abandonment of a grammatical construction, an abandonment signifying a shift or break in thought. Use dashes to set off an emphatic parenthetical insertion.

And then I—but who cares?

And then Simon Pure—what a shock to us all—said his first and last unprintable word.

If a parenthetical remark that would otherwise be set off by commas contains commas, you may need to use the dash to prevent confusion. Notice how bewildering it is to read the following: "The Seven Deadly Sins, pride, lechery, envy, anger, covetousness, gluttony, and sloth, are exactly what make life worth living." Better: "The Seven Deadly Sins—pride, lechery, envy, anger, covetousness, gluttony, and sloth—are exactly what make life worth living."

4.5   The Ellipsis

The ellipsis marks either an omission from a quoted passage or an uncompleted sentence. The latest *MLA Style Manual and Guide to Scholarly Publishing* recommends that the ellipsis always be used with brackets when it marks an omission from a quoted passage. At least one textual aesthete holds that bracketed ellipses produce graceless pages, but he grants that the practice holds some advantages over using ellipses without brackets. Section 4.5.1 details the latest MLA recommendations. Section 4.5.2 details the older conventions for using the ellipsis. The older conventions are still used by many publications and continue to be proper for marking uncompleted sentences that are not part of a quoted passage.

4.5.1   Ellipsis with brackets

The basic bracketed ellipsis is given thus:

  [. . .]

The central period is flanked by spaces, but there are no spaces between a bracket and its adjacent period. The bracketed ellipsis may mark the omission of the beginning of a quoted sentence:

  "[. . .] I saw; I conquered."

The bracketed ellipsis may mark an omission within a quoted sentence:

  "I came [. . .] I conquered."

There are single spaces before the first bracket and after the second. The ellipsis overrides interior punctuation, here eliminating the semicolon following "came" and that preceding "I conquered."

A bracketed ellipsis may also appear at the end of a quotation:

"I came; I saw [. . .]."

Again the bracketed ellipsis overrides interior punctuation, the semicolon after "saw." The bracketed ellipsis is followed without a space by the period at the end of the quoted sentence. If, though, the quoting writer ends the sentence with a parenthetical reference, the end punctuation follows the quotation marks and the parenthesis:

"I came; I saw [. . .]" (27).

The bracketed ellipsis is also used to indicate the omission of one or more sentences. When so used, the ellipsis must be flanked by complete sentences (composed completely of quoted matter or composed of a combination of quoted matter and the writer's own words):

> Poetry deals with primal and conventional things—the hunger for bread, the love of woman, the love of children, the desire for immortal life. [. . .] It is original, not in the paltry sense of being new, but in the deeper sense of being old; it is original in the sense that it deals with origins. (G. K. Chesterton)

This construction includes an extra, double space at the end of the ellipsis. Double-space between sentences, even when the earlier sentence ends with an ellipsis.

The sentence period is always logically placed with respect to the bracketed ellipsis. In the quotation given above, the first sentence ends with "life," so the period follows immediately. If the first sentence had continued after "life," the punctuation at the ellipsis would have been given thus: "life [. . .]. It is original."

An ellipsis can also mark an omission that runs from the middle of one sentence to the middle of the next sentence or even a later one.

Blanched Sun,—blighted grass,—blinded man
[. . .] [T]he Empire of England, on which for-
merly the sun never set, has become one on which
he never rises. (John Ruskin)

The lack of a sentence period before or after the bracketed ellipsis could indicate that the quotation is drawn
from a single sentence, or it could indicate (as is the case
here) that it is drawn from two that are not adjacent.

Finally, when giving an indented quotation of verse, signify the omission of one or more complete lines by
bracketing spaced periods in a line as long as the lines of
verse quoted:

As monk to cell he seeks this stall
For soul and body's sake: to purge
The flesh, illuminate the wall,
Both nature's and creation's urge.
[. . . . .]
And writes upon the wall his name,
For one to him are shame and fame.
(Walker Gibson)

4.5.2   Ellipsis without brackets

To mark an uncompleted sentence or to use the older
method to mark an omission from a quoted passage, use
the ellipsis without brackets. The ellipsis consists of
three spaced periods—a total of three periods and four
spaces:

#.#.#.#

Here each pound sign stands for a space. Everything is
part of the ellipsis, including the single spaces with
which the ellipsis begins and ends. However, when the
ellipsis comes just before or just after a quotation mark,
the ellipsis loses its space next to the quotation mark. In
other words, there is no space between a quotation mark
and the nearest period of an adjacent ellipsis:

>". . . from these honored dead we take increased devotion to that cause for which they gave the last full measure of devotion . . ." (Abraham Lincoln).

An ellipsis may mark the omission of the beginning of a quoted sentence:

>". . . I saw; I conquered."

An ellipsis may mark an omission within a quoted sentence:

>"I came . . . I conquered."

The ellipsis overrides interior punctuation, here eliminating the semicolon following "came" and that preceding "I conquered."

An ellipsis may also appear at the end of a quotation:

>"I came; I saw. . . ."

An ellipsis does not override end punctuation, either that of the quoted sentence or that of the quoting writer's sentence. The first period (here enlarged) in the previous example is the end punctuation of the sentence—here the period marking the end of the quoting writer's own sentence. There is no space between the final word of the quoted sentence and the end punctuation. Rather than preceding the end punctuation, as logic would dictate, the ellipsis proper follows the end punctuation. If, though, the quoting writer ends the sentence with a parenthetical reference, the ellipsis is the standard, three-period one, and the end punctuation follows the closed parenthesis:

>"I came; I saw . . ." (27).

The four-period ellipsis is also used within a quoted passage, to indicate the omission of one or more sentences. When so used, the ellipsis must be flanked by complete sentences (composed completely of quoted matter or composed of a combination of quoted matter and the writer's own words):

> Poetry deals with primal and conventional things—the hunger for bread, the love of woman, the love of children, the desire for immortal life. . . . It is original, not in the paltry sense of being new, but in the deeper sense of being old; it is original in the sense that it deals with origins. (G. K. Chesterton)

This construction includes an extra, double space at the end of the ellipsis. Double-space between sentences, even when the earlier sentence ends with an ellipsis.

Finally, when giving an indented quotation of verse, signify the omission of one or more complete lines by typing spaced periods in a line as long as the lines of verse quoted:

> As monk to cell he seeks this stall
> For soul and body's sake: to purge
> The flesh, illuminate the wall,
> Both nature's and creation's urge.
> . . . .
> And writes upon the wall his name,
> For one to him are shame and fame.
>
>   (Walker Gibson)

4.6 The Exclamation Point

The exclamation point marks exclamations, and that is all it does. It is the loudest, laziest member of the punctuation family. It is almost always awkward and out of its element in expository prose. Formal prose welcomes passion, but only when escorted by eloquence, and the exclamation point is rarely the mark of eloquence. Unless you wish to sound like Sis Boombah, use sparingly. Sparingly!

4.7 | **The Hyphen**

Distinguish between the hyphen and the dash. Although similar in form, they differ in function. The hyphen is not just a stunted, abortive dash, but a mark in its own right.

The hyphen is used for a number of very different purposes.

4.7.1   Use the hyphen to divide a word too long to fit at the end of a line. Split such a word between syllables, placing the first part of the word at the end of the line and the remainder at the beginning of the next line (words of one syllable, no matter how long—*strengths*, for instance—may not be so divided). Place a hyphen immediately after the first segment. To ascertain that you are dividing the word between syllables, see your dictionary, which gives the syllables of a word thus: sen•ti•men•tal•i•ty.

There are two refinements upon such word division: (a) Do not divide a word leaving only one or two letters for the beginning of a new line (for example, do not divide the following words thus: exhib-it, expeditious-ly, delight-ed. And (b) Divide an already hyphenated word at the hyphen only. For example, divide *bluish-green* after the *h* but not after the *u*.

4.7.2   Use the hyphen to join two or more words serving as a single adjective preceding its noun: "a half-hearted wish," "an as-good-as-gold guarantee," "the dog-tired crew," "a reddish-brown mineral." When the formation comes after its noun, it is not hyphenated: "This guarantee is as good as gold"; "The mineral is reddish brown."

Exception: if the adjectival cluster contains an adverb ending in *ly*, do not hyphenate after the adverb: "a reddish-brown mineral," but "a mostly brown mineral."

4.7.3   Use the hyphen to join two-word numbers between twenty-one and ninety-nine. Use the hyphen to join fractions used as adjectives, but not fractions used as nouns: "forty-two," "three hundred forty-two," a three-fourths majority," "three fourths of the members," "thirty-four of the members."

4.7.4 Use an open-ended hyphen to punctuate constructions like the following one: "You may choose the six-, eight-, or ten-year plan."

Note that many words regularly take a hyphen: *cross-link*, for example, but not *crossroad* or *cross section*. Your dictionary will help you determine whether a word takes the hyphen. Some typical ones that do: *x-ray, U-turn, self-appointed, ex-convict, wishy-washy, anti-Semitic* (but not *antiseptic*). Be careful not to confuse pairs like *re-creation* and *recreation*, *coop* and *co-op*.

4.8   **Parentheses**

Parentheses are verbal jailers. They segregate and repress. Ruthless but useful, they minimize the impact of potentially unruly and disruptive words (or numerals) that nevertheless serve a purpose in the sentence. Commas or dashes can also segregate, but not with the repressive power of parentheses. See 3.6.

The chief difficulty with parentheses is integrating them with other marks of punctuation. Whenever the portion of the sentence preceding the parentheses would ordinarily be followed by a punctuation mark, place the mark after the closing parenthesis.

> Bubba Smith's favorite English poet is Mary Elizabeth Coleridge (1861-1907), the great-grandniece of Samuel Taylor Coleridge (1772-1834).

There is one exception—quotation marks:

> John Ruskin called engraving "the Art of Scratch" (*Ariadne Florentina*, 1873-76).

See chapter 7 for other stylistic conventions pertaining to quotation. If you place an entire sentence in parentheses, punctuate in either of the following ways:

> "No ladyfingers for me, thank you," replied Igor (he had stopped for lunch along the way).

"No ladyfingers for me, thank you," replied Igor. (**He** had stopped for lunch along the way**.**)

The second form calls more attention to the parenthetical matter than the first does, offsetting somewhat the repressive function of its parentheses. The first form is therefore usually preferable, because not at cross-purposes with itself.

4.9 | **The Period**

4.9.1 Place a period at the end of most sentences. Declarative sentences, imperative sentences unless passionately uttered, indirect questions, and direct questions that are imperative in force all take the period.

> All art is quite useless.
> (Oscar Wilde)   *[declarative sentence]*
>
> Look before you creep.   *[imperative sentence]*
>
> He wondered whether Delta House could preserve its reputation for refined elegance.
>   *[indirect question]*
>
> Would you be so kind as to remove your sneaker from my chest.   *[imperative question]*

4.9.2 Use the period to indicate most abbreviations.

> Dr. Ms. Bart. Feb. etc.

Some abbreviations, however, do not take a period.

> DAR FBI CIA MP USMA

Your trusty dictionary will inform you which abbreviations require a period, which do not, and which may be written in either fashion.

4.10 | **The Question Mark**

The question mark does only one thing: it marks direct questions. Use the question mark for internal as well as terminal punctuation:

> Well, if it isn't—do my eyes deceive me?—Michael Jordan!

> Were the creatures from the alien spacecraft magenta?

See 4.9 ("The Period") for punctuating indirect questions.

See 4.11 ("Quotation Marks") for placement of the question mark in punctuating quotations.

4.11 | **Quotation Marks**

4.11.1 | Use quotation marks to frame direct quotations presented as part of your own lines of prose. *Indented* direct quotations do not take quotation marks, for the indentation suffices to show direct quotation. Nor do *indirect* quotations take quotation marks:

> The apoplectic swami screamed at the hecklers that he had long since achieved perfect tranquillity.

Distinguish between letters, numerals, single words, or longer units given as quoted and given as such. The first are marked by quotation marks; the second, by italics (or underlining):

> Margo said that she wanted to "rap" some more.

> No one uses <u>rap</u> anymore.

This distinction and those of 4.11.2 and 4.11.3 are discussed more extensively under "Italics," 5.3.

4.11.2 Use italics (or underlining) for a term being defined, quotation marks for its meaning:

> To rap is outmoded slang for "to converse informally and intimately."

4.11.3 Distinguish, too, between titles of shorter genres (essays, articles, chapters, short stories, songs, and most poems) and titles of longer genres (books, newspapers, magazines, plays, movies, and very long poems). The first are framed in quotation marks; the second, italicized.

4.11.4 Use single quotation marks ('. . .') to indicate a direct quotation within a direct quotation. Otherwise use double quotation marks wherever quotation marks are called for.

> "Which of you young scholars," asked Professor Vellum, "has quoted Tennyson's Ulysses as saying, 'I am become a name, / For always roaming with a hungry hart'?"

4.11.5 Most grammatical problems with quotation marks involve the placement of other marks in relation to them. For using a comma or a colon **to introduce a quotation**, see 7.2.2. For punctuation **at the end of a quotation**, see what follows. American usage is fairly simple and consistent, although not always logical. Whenever the choice presents itself,

- Place a period or comma inside the quotation marks. If, however, a parenthesis immediately follows the quotation, the period or comma follows the parenthesis.

- Always place a colon or semicolon outside the quotation marks.

- Place a question mark or exclamation point inside or outside, on the basis of whether the mark punctuates the quoted matter or the larger sentence.

> Nelly insists that Heathcliff is "a human being," but later she considers him "a ghoul, or a vampire."
>
> Nelly insists that Heathcliff is "a human being" (143), but later she considers him "a ghoul, or a vampire" (260).
>
> Once we were "living in sin," then "having an affair"; now we are "involved in a relationship."
>
> Is America no longer the "home of the brave"?
>
> She wondered, "Why does no one these days want to grow up to be a saint?"

- Whenever more than one of these six marks are called for at the end of a quotation, let a single mark stand for all. One period or comma will do for two, and one of the four larger marks will drive out a period or comma. For example, although logic would dictate a period at the end of the last-quoted sentence, the question mark of the quotation subsumes the period.

4.11.6   Another, questionable use of quotation marks is flagging a word or phrase as disowned even as it is adopted.

> Luke Warm is not a "gutsy" fullback.

It is always better to use words you are willing to stand behind. If *gutsy* makes you squeamish, use *tough, aggressive*, or *daring*. Use *plucky*, which sounds more genteel, but only because people have forgotten its literal meaning, which is exactly that of *gutsy*. Use the less modish *gutty*. Call gutless Luke a coward or quitter, if you dare. But do avoid *intestinal fortitude*, which is simply inflated old guts with no zing left in them—more paunch than punch. Finally, if the low company and present overuse of *gutsy* do not deter you, why not say

> Luke Warm is not a gutsy fullback.

and let readers tut and twitter if they will. By taking full responsibility for your own words, you will be being gutsy.

4.12   **The Semicolon**

The semicolon is badly named. It behaves not at all like a colon. The forward-facing colon proclaims some coming event; the semicolon, pointing in opposite directions simultaneously, both divides and joins two syntactically equal sentence-units. Names more descriptive of the semicolon's function would be the "double comma" or the "semiperiod." Although the comma or period is almost always a better choice than the semicolon, two definable conditions cry out for the semicolon instead.

4.12.1   Use the semicolon to mark a series of terms that themselves contain commas. With commas in place of the following semicolons, the major and minor series would become confused with one another:

> Would you rather bring the hot dogs, hamburgers, and cold cuts; the bread, rolls, lettuce, tomatoes, and cucumbers; or the potato chips, beer, and soft drinks?

4.12.2   Use the semicolon as a terse, forceful way to imply a strong similarity or sharp contrast between independent clauses. Often the clauses thus joined are similar in sentence structure and wording. Often, too, for greater terseness, the second clause omits terms the reader must supply from the first clause. Whenever the semicolon joins independent clauses, it vouches for their equality and close relationship.

> There were a king with a large jaw and a queen with a plain face on the throne of England; there were a king with a large jaw and a queen with a fair face on the throne of France. (Charles Dickens)

> Instead of three meals a day, if it be necessary, eat but one; instead of a hundred dishes, five [. . .]. (Henry David Thoreau)

At work he is a lion; at home, a polecat.

If neither of these conditions exists, you are almost always right to avoid the semicolon. In the following sentence, for example, the semicolon reneges on its promise of close relationship between clauses, betraying the reader:

I do not know why I came to UConn; I have enjoyed the dairy bar, which serves large portions of good ice cream.

4.12.3   Because a semicolon announces a balance of equals, do not use a semicolon to join syntactically unequal constructions.

Wrong: After Al Legro had sung "Vaga luna," by Bellini; Anne Dante played Chopin's Sonata No. 2 in B-Flat Minor.

Wrong: Under the far corner of the lavender rug on the floor of the room at the end of the hall on the third floor of the dormitory at the top of the hill at the University of Connecticut; the roach led a modest but happy existence.

In the first example the semicolon wrongly joins an adverb clause to a main clause; in the second, the semicolon wrongly joins a festoon of twelve prepositional phrases to a main clause. Neither pairing produces the balance of equals that the semicolon promises.

4.13   The Slash

Use the slash—or, to give it its proper name, the virgule—with a clear conscience to separate quoted lines of poetry run into your text rather than indented: "Still round and round the ghosts of beauty glide, / And haunt the places where their honor died." Observe the single spaces fore and aft the slash. Also use the slash *without* spacing to type fractions given in numerals (*1/4*) and, in linguistics, to set off phonemic transcriptions.

Although the slash has become modish (see, for example, *and/or*, *his/her*), it remains in bad odor when applied to uses other than the three just mentioned. Perhaps its ill repute is due to its always leaping out from a page of prose and disrupting it, much like those other untamed creatures of the keys @, #, +, %, &, and *. Besides, the slash, which calls to mind computers, robots, and Leonard Nimoy, suggests that the author who favors it aspires to the humanoid. Then, too, the reader is seldom sure whether a writer intends a slash to mean *and, or*, or both. *And/or* looks very sure of itself, but it only multiplies the uncertainty. By saying simply "and" or "or" instead, you gain precision and strike a blow for humanity.

5. Other Conventions of Writing: Abbreviation; Capitalization; Italics; Numbers

Like punctuation, the conventions discussed in this chapter apply to writing but not to speech. No matter how fluently and cogently one talks, to be adept at putting words on paper, one must learn not only how and when to punctuate but also how and when to abbreviate, to capitalize, to italicize, and to write numbers.

5.1

Abbreviation

Merely because an abbreviation exists, it may not be used just anywhere. Words and terms may be divided into three categories: those that have no standard abbreviation, those that are unabbreviated except under very limited circumstances, and those whose abbreviation is appropriate and even preferable in almost all circumstances.

5.1.1 Unabbreviated Words

The first category includes almost all words. Almost all words should be unabbreviated when written for a general readership. Of course, diarists or pen pals may develop a set of private conventions that includes unconventional abbreviation, and a shopper's list may consist of "brd, bttr, mlk, lgtblbs." Such private correspondence is nobody else's business.

Words susceptible to inappropriate abbreviation include

corporation	Avoid using *corp.* unless it is part of a title, as in *Bon Mot Manufacturing Corp.*
brother	Avoid using *bros.* unless it is part of a title, as in *Dingaling Bros. Circus.*
company	Avoid using *co.* unless it is part of a title, as in *Cosmic Frisbee Co.*
incorporated	Avoid using *inc.* unless it is part of a title, as in *Top Dog Dating Service, Inc.*

5.1.2   Occasionally Abbreviated Words

The second category includes many table- or chart-words, which are abbreviated on maps, charts, tables, calendars, and other close-set text but are spelled out in ordinary discourse.

and *and* & *(the ampersand)*

Sunday *and* Sun.

August *and* Aug.

Mountain *and* Mt.

Avenue *and* Ave.

pounds *and* lbs.

inches *and* in.

feet *and* ft.

page(s) *and* p(p).

volume(s) *and* vol(s).

chapter(s) *and* ch(s).

number(s) *and* no(s).

New Jersey *and* NJ

teaspoon(s) *and* tsp(s).

Some titles fall into this category. The titles are abbreviated when they introduce a proper name but are spelled in full when used generally:

Mr. Meanor	Mister, can you spare twenty dollars?
Dr. Ripoff	Is there a doctor in the house?

Many other titles, though, are not abbreviated; they belong in our first category. These titles include most academic, military, governmental, and religious titles:

Professor Notabene (*not* Prof. Notabene)

General Paresis (*not* Gen. Paresis)

Senator Pulsetaker (*not* Sen. Pulsetaker)

the Reverend Benjamin Dictus (*not* Rev. Dictus)

If an academic, military, governmental, or religious title consists of more than one word, it may be abbreviated if it introduces a full name—both given name and surname.

Pfc. [Private, First Class] Beetle Bailey is long overdue for a demotion.

Rt. Rev. Msgr. [The Right Reverend Monsignor] Oliver Pruitt refused to sign the petition.

Although *saint* may be unabbreviated or abbreviated when used as a title, many stylists prefer the word unabbreviated.

St. Nicholas *or, better*, Saint Nicholas

Finally, *Dr., Mr., Mrs.*, or *Ms* is dropped if another title (except *Jr.* or *Sr.*) is used. And the doctor, professor, or president is rare who welcomes being called "Doc," "Prof," or "Prez."

5.1.3 Usually Abbreviated Words

The third category includes titles following a name

Jr.	Sr.
MD	DMD
DDS	PhD
SJ	EdD
OBE	Bart.

words used with dates

BC	AD

10 a.m. (*or* AM)

familiar acronyms (abbreviations pronounced as a word)

GOP	NATO
TNT	USA
IBM	NASA
NBC	UNESCO

and some Latin (or other foreign) expressions used as textual signals:

i.e. (*id est*): that is to say

e.g. (*exempli gratia*): for example

cf. (*confer*): compare

NB (*nota bene*): notice

etc. (*et cetera*): and so forth

et al. (*et alii*): and others

These last abbreviations should be reserved for foot-notes and parentheses. In normal text, use an unabbreviated English equivalent. For example, use *for example* rather than *e.g.*

The trend is away from using periods in abbreviations. Most abbreviations that consist of or end in capital letters take no periods. Most that consist of or end in lower-case letters do, however. Your best guide is a recently published desk dictionary.

5.2 Capitalization

The first letter of a proper noun is capitalized. The first letter of a common noun is not, unless the noun begins a sentence or appears in the title of an essay, book, play, or any other work of art.

Proper here does not mean "correct." Instead it keeps its old, Latin meaning, "one's own." A proper noun is a name peculiar to the thing named—the thing's very own name. A proper noun refers to a class of one. A common noun, on the other hand, refers to a class of more than one.

Publius Ovidius Naso is a proper noun: there is only one Publius Ovidius Naso. *Ann Smith* is also a proper noun. Although there are many Ann Smiths in the world, out of courtesy we use the term as if there were only one. Even *Ann* is a proper noun, for the same reason. If, on the other hand, we refer to Publius Ovidius Naso as "the banished poet," we are considering him as a member of a larger class, even if he is the only member of that class who comes to mind. The great majority of nouns and noun phrases are, of course, common.

A common noun can become proper by serving as part of a proper term. The word *professor* is a common noun, for it refers to an all-too-large class of people. But when the word takes its place in a title—Professor Vellum—it helps to compose a term referring to a class of one. *Professor* is, therefore, capitalized when so used.

There are a few exceptions to these conventions: the days of the week and the months are capitalized, although there are many Fridays and Februaries. The four seasons, though, are not capitalized. And a few titles, although common, are capitalized in honor of the office.

The **Czar** of Russia

The **President** of the United States

The **Queen** of England

Some words other than nouns are capitalized: the pronoun *I*, for instance, and the old-fashioned pronoun *O* (as in "O Caesar"). And some adjectives formed from proper nouns are also capitalized: *Victorian, Dickensian, Jacksonian, Shavian.* As the centuries pass, such adjectives tend to settle into lower-case words: *sadistic, herculean, satanic.* If unsure whether such an adjective is capitalized, look it up in your dictionary.

Finally, words of any of the eight parts of speech are capitalized when they meet any one of four conditions:

• They begin a sentence.

• They are the first or last word in the title of an essay, book, play, or any other work of art.

• They are the first word after a colon or semicolon in such a title.

- They are one of the other, interior words in such a title, unless they are an article, the *to* of the infinitive, a preposition, or a coordinating conjunction.

5.3   **Italics**

Italic type is thin, slanted type, whereas normal, Roman type is thicker and vertical. The printer of a book or magazine changes type to display true italics; the writer using a typewriter or pen uses underlining to signify italics; the printer of a newspaper, who ordinarily uses neither italic type nor underlining, resorts to quotation marks to signify italics. Most writers, therefore, underline to signify italics. And it is a good idea for students submitting an academic paper produced on a computer to use underlining for italics. Although underlining is not so pretty as true italics, it stands out in the text more clearly. Therefore, for the sake of clarity I use underlining in the rest of this section to mark italics.

Although italics are sometimes used for mere emphasis, a better way to go about stressing a term is through the apt choice and arrangement of one's words. Italicizing for mere emphasis tends to make the writer seem strident or gushy. Moreover, the practice interferes with the special uses of italics.

5.3.1   Use italics to refer to a word or term itself rather than to what it denotes.

It would, for instance, be incorrect, because confusing, to write

> Septimus is the name of one of Tennyson's brothers.

The person and the word get in each other's way. But neither of the following sentences causes this confusion:

> Septimus is one of Tennyson's brothers.

> <u>Septimus</u> is the name of one of Tennyson's brothers.

In the second example italics signal the reader to consider momentarily the word itself, not its meaning. Here are some additional examples:

> I want you home by midnight—no *if*'s, *and*'s, or *but*'s.

> He pronounced *success* with a slight lisp.

5.3.2   Use italics to refer to a numeral, alphabetical letter, or typographical mark itself rather than to what it denotes.

Distinguish between

> I counted 143 paper clips.

and

> Scrawled across the bottom of the page was a string of *143*s.

The first example uses *143* normally, for what it means; the second example presents the number as an object and, by giving it in italics, cues the reader to consider it as such. Here are some further examples of such usage:

> He pronounced the word with a slight *th*-sound.

> Minding your *p*'s and *q*'s is never so easy as *abc*.

> Avoid using *&* unless it is part of a title.

If words or terms as such are given in roman type (as in indented examples), true italics may be used for words used normally. Under these conditions italics and roman type exchange functions:

> **Example:** to perspire freely, *not* to freely perspire

5.3.3   If quoting to indicate the term itself, use italics; if quoting to indicate the term's meaning, use quotation marks.

In quoting, a writer necessarily refers to words, terms, numerals, letters, or typographical marks. In deciding between quotation marks and italics for marking quoted terms, decide whether the term is introduced for the sake of the quoted term itself or for the sake of its meaning. If the term itself, use italics; if the meaning, use quotation marks.

> Whenever Hiram says "Scat!" his hounds know he has had a hard day.

> Whenever Hiram says *scat*, he uses the word in the full knowledge that it is derived from a hissing sound plus *cat*.

Because writers almost always quote for the sake of meaning rather than wording, quoted terms are almost always given in quotation marks rather than in italics. In doubtful cases, the longer the quoted term, the better the odds that it should be given in quotation marks. If still in doubt, use quotation marks, on the grounds that the reader will be more familiar and, therefore, more comfortable with them.

5.3.4   In a definition the term being defined is given in italics, its meaning in quotation marks:

> *Migraine* is derived from a Greek word, *hemikrania*, which means "half the skull."

5.3.5   Use italics to mark the longer form of a type whose shorter form is given in quotation marks.

In other situations, too, italics and quotation marks rub elbows, but the line between them is more easily drawn. Italics and quotation marks serve together to differentiate between longer and shorter forms of similar types.

The longer forms are given in italics; the shorter, in quotation marks.

- The title of a novel or other book is given in italics:

    The Mayor of Casterbridge [novel]

    Lolita [novel]

    Civilization and Its Discontents [expository book]

    Gulliver's Travels [novel]

    But the title of a short story or essay is given in quotation marks:

    "A Modest Proposal" [essay]

    "Hills Like White Elephants" [short story]

- The title of a magazine or newspaper is given in italics:

    Newsweek [magazine]

    Journal of English and Germanic Philology [scholarly journal]

    The New York Times [newspaper]

    the London *Times* [newspaper]

    the Willimantic *Chronicle* [newspaper]

(The name of the city in which a newspaper is published may or may not be part of the newspaper's title. The name plate of the newspaper, displayed at the top of the first page, will include the name of the city if the name is part of the newspaper's title.)

But the title of an article published in a magazine or newspaper is given in quotation marks:

"Sox Drop Another" [newspaper story]

"Browning's Witless Duke" [essay in journal of literature]

- The title of a poem published as a volume is given in italics:

Paradise Lost

Modern Love

The Waste Land

But the title of a poem published within a larger work (e.g., a volume of poetry or a magazine) is given in quotation marks:

"The Emperor of Ice Cream"

"The Bird with the Coppery, Keen Claws"

- The title of a long musical work is given in italics unless the title is simply a statement of the work's genre, number, and key:

Ein Heldenleben [a symphonic work]

Tosca [an opera]

Chopin's Sonata No. 2 in B-Flat Minor

But the title of a song is given in quotation marks:

"Be My Love" [popular old song]

"In a Pawnshop on a Corner in Pittsburgh, Pennsylvania" [not-very-popular old song]

- The title of a television or radio program is given in italics:

  Old Ma Perkins [old radio program]

  Dragnet [old television program]

  The Howdy Doody Show [old television program]

  But that of an individual episode is given in quotation marks:

  "The Hairball Murders of Horsley Woodhouse" [mystery episode]

  "The Fonz Scores Again" [old Happy Days episode]

5.3.6   Use italics to mark words of a few additional types.

- The title of a play

  Androcles and the Lion [play]

  The Importance of Being Earnest [play]

- The title of a movie

  The Texas Chainsaw Massacre

  Beat the Devil

  My Brilliant Career

- The title of a painting, statue, or other work of visual art

  Guernica [painting]

  The Thinker [statue]

- The name of a ship, airplane, train, or other large vehicle

    <u>Wabash Cannonball</u> [train]

    <u>the Titanic</u> [ship]

    <u>H.M.S. Pinafore</u> [fictitious ship]

    <u>Winnie Mae</u> [old, once-famous airplane]

    <u>Millennium Falcon</u> [fictitious spaceship]

- Foreign terms not yet blended into the English vocabulary

    Adding whipped cream to that rich dessert is <u>de trop</u>.

    The very first MacDonald's hamburger joint has been torn down: <u>sic transit gloria mundi</u>.

Italics reassure readers that foreign terms are indeed foreign. Generally, though, the need for reassurance should not arise: readers who know what a foreign term means do not have to be told that it is foreign, and readers who do not know what it means should be spared an incomprehensible polyglot performance. As a rule, use foreign terms familiar to speakers of English—terms that do not need to be italicized:

kibbutz	hacienda
rendezvous	blasé
menage	mea culpa
élan	chic
a priori	hara-kiri
prima donna	sukiyaki

If, however, you know that your reader will understand you and if there is no English equivalent, use the foreign term. Dictionaries mark all foreign expressions as such. If an expression is marked as foreign and if you decide to use it, italicize it.

5.3.7   Exceptions

- A work's own title, written at the head of the text, is not given in italics or quotation marks.

- The Bible and the books of the Bible are not given in italics or quotation marks.

5.4   Numbers

In tables, graphs, endnotes or footnotes, bibliographies, maps, charts, recipes, and anywhere else where compactness is especially important, give all numbers as numerals. In standard prose spell out a number that can be given in one or two words, give the numeral for one that cannot. For the sake of uniformity, however, once you give one number in numerals, use numerals for all numbers in the passage.

twenty-four blackbirds

three thousand tarts

294 spelling errors

101 phoebes and 24 red-winged blackbirds

The trend is away from numbers as words and toward numbers as numerals. Some writers now write as numerals all numbers of ten and over. For the time being, though, let the number of words in a number determine how you write it.

Numerals may *always* be used in giving the following information. These numerals do not require the writer to change all other numbers in a passage to numerals:

- Times of day

    12:47 P.M.

- Dates

    April 11, 1936

- Addresses

    19 Pokeberry Lane

- Chapters and pages of a book

    Chapter 99; page 3

- Acts, scenes, and lines of a play

    Act 5; scene 8; line 12; 5.8.12

- Sections, stanzas, and lines of a poem

    Section 4; stanza 16; lines 12 to 17; 4.16.12-17

- Decimals

    12.5389

- Fractions

    9 3/4

- Percentages

    75 percent; 75 %

- Scores of games

    The Cardinals beat the Mets 17 to 1.

- Proper names that include numerals

    Route 44

Channel 3

Pope John Paul II

It is in keeping with the conventions just mentioned to say either

I shall meet you at nine o'clock.

or

I shall meet you at 9:00.

Numerals are correct for the second sentence because *9:00*, which gives minutes as well as the hour, cannot be stated fully in two words or fewer. The time given in the second sentence is more specific than that given in the first. *O'clock* should always be accompanied by the time given in words rather than in numerals.

Do not use a numeral to begin a sentence. If the numeral is otherwise appropriate at the beginning of a sentence, do not give the number in words but postpone the number by rephrasing the sentence.

Wrong: 1642 was not the best year for rhubarb.

Wrong: Sixteen forty-two was not the best year for rhubarb.

Right: The best year for rhubarb was not 1642.

6. Plagiarism

This chapter and the next three chapters discuss using the ideas of one person in the writing of another. This chapter distinguishes between ethically proper and improper ways of doing so. Chapter 7, "Quotation," describes stylistically proper ways of incorporating the words of one writer into the text of another. Then chapters 8 and 9 describe stylistically proper ways of acknowledging one's use of the words, ideas, and findings of others.

In at least one way an academic course is like the Garden of Eden: one finds there just one act absolutely forbidden. The act is plagiarism: presenting the perceptions, phrasing, or train of thought of another as one's own. It is stealing and lying simultaneously.

Some people see nothing wrong with plagiarism. They have never learned to treasure ideas of their own—have never experienced the joy of intellectual creation. Their blindness is often due to faulty schooling, which stressed the parroting of others' ideas at the expense of creative consideration. Whatever the cause of their problem, they are to be pitied rather than condemned.

Pride in and respect for ideas is the basis for the code observed by all true thinkers (a community extending far beyond the university). True thinkers may disagree bitterly, may dislike one another personally, but they act together to preserve the integrity of ideas. Part of the code consists of acknowledging the author and written source of a borrowed idea. Part consists of distinguishing between an idea in its original form and the idea as recast by the borrower. These customs—notation and quotation—create the largest communications network ever, dwarfing the World Wide Web by extending not only around the globe but also back through time.

Because plagiarists violate the code and disrupt the network, they are anathema to thinkers. Few students plagiarize intentionally. But others do so inadvertently, finding the dividing line between plagiarism and the reporting of others' ideas hard to draw. The line is hard to draw. Therefore I elaborate on what is plagiarism and what is not.

If you include the words or ideas of others in a work you publish for financial profit, you must observe copyright laws, which I do not discuss here. But if you write an essay for a course (or for a journal that does not pay you for your essay), you may include any aspect of any writer's work as long as you acknowledge the source. Borrow anything but acknowledge all you borrow.

It is obvious that copying the work of another and then presenting the copy as your own work is plagiarism. Even if you were to buy an essay from a mail-order research company and submit it as your own work, you would still be committing plagiarism. Your payment to the company would entitle you to own the document but not to transmit it as your creation. Any financial arrangement with a research outfit is irrelevant to the ethical obligation to your reader. Needless to say, the same argument applies to papers written by one student and submitted by another as original work.

Recasting without acknowledgment the ideas of another into your own words is also plagiarism. The following examples of the practice are not fictitious; they are taken from a paper of a former student. For obvious reasons I here disobey my own rule in not citing the source. The plagiarized passages are based on Walter Harding, *Henry David Thoreau's* Walden *and* Civil Disobedience: *A Study Guide*, Bound Brook, NJ: Shelley, 1962:

Harding:	Thoreau's vocabulary is large. He will send every conscientious student to the dictionary again and again.
Essay:	Thoreau's word-choice is precise, but his large vocabulary makes a dictionary a necessity.
Harding:	Thoreau's appeal to reduce life to its essentials, to get down to the very marrow of life, has increased [*Walden's*] potency and charm.
Essay:	*Walden* deals with understanding life by reducing it to the basic level.
Harding:	Thomas Wentworth Higginson, one of the minor Transcendentalists, once said a good many years ago that *Walden* was one of the few American books worth re-reading every year.
Essay:	I can now understand why a former teacher of mine praised Walden as "the only book worth re-reading once a year."

Even when someone else's ideas or phrases are transferred to a new area of thought, the source should be acknowledged. Suppose, for instance, that a student writing on Molière's *Tartuffe* is reminded of W. H. Auden's description of comedy as "good tempered and pessimistic—it believes that we cannot change human nature and must make the best of a bad job" ("Byron: The Making of a Comic Poet," *New York Review of Books* 18 Aug. 1966: 13). The student can legitimately apply Auden's idea to Molière's play, for the application is the student's own idea. But he should not proceed to write about Molière's "sunny resignation" without acknowledging the debt to Auden. Similarly, suppose that a reader of W. V. Quine and J. S. Sullivan's *The Web of Belief* (New York: Random, 1970) is drawn to the remark "Everyday terms are mainly suited for everyday affairs, where lax talk is rife" (66). If that reader were to go on to write without attribution, "George Eliot chronicles humdrum life, where lax talk is rife," she would be plagiarizing, despite the fresh setting for the clause. She would be implicitly claiming as her own not only the words but also the urbane ease that deftly utters much in five off-hand monosyllables.

Acknowledgment is unnecessary, though, when a borrowing will be evident to the reader. No reader needs to be told that Shakespeare's *Hamlet* is the source for "To be or not to be," that the Oedipus complex is a Freudian concept, or that "Nice guys finish last" is the wisdom of Leo Durocher. In essays written for a course, you need not tell your professors which ideas are reflections of their own. But whenever you are unsure whether a source will be recognized, cite it.

Much of what you find in encyclopedias or in the editor's notes to your texts consists of general knowledge. Consider, for instance, these remarks:

> When Chaucer's Pandarus declares, "I have a jolly woe, a lusty sorrow," he is availing himself of the classical rhetorical device *oxymoron*.

> A Spenserian stanza consists of nine lines rhyming *ababbcbcc*, the first eight lines being iambic pentameter and the final line an iambic hexameter (an *alexandrine*).

> Nathaniel Hawthorne admired the novels of Anthony Trollope.

The remarks may be news to many people, but they will be stale fare to anyone familiar with the authors mentioned. The source of such preliminary, background information—whatever will not impress your teacher as original thinking—probably need not be cited. But if you reproduce a great deal of such stock information or if some such fact is crucial in establishing your own idea, then do mention your source.

All said thus far can be summarized in two simple rules: First, acknowledge anything borrowed that might be mistaken for your own. Second, acknowledge even an obvious borrowing when your original idea relies heavily on it.

Penalties. At the University of Connecticut a student found guilty of plagiarism receives an *F* for the course and is reported to the Division of Student Personnel. An accomplice—someone who intentionally writes a paper for another or who lets another copy his work—is considered equally guilty and is liable to the same penalties.

To give students whose instructor have judged them guilty the opportunity to present their case to a third party, the English Department has named a Committee of Review, composed of members of the department. A student who feels unjustly accused of plagiarism may apply to the committee for a hearing. Other departments have instituted similar committees and procedures, as has the Department of Student Affairs.

7. Quotation

Purposes and proprieties.

Quotation serves two different purposes: First, when discussing a written work, essayists quote to present evidence for their own perceptions. And second, they quote to acknowledge precisely their debt to other thinkers. Because commentators on literature are always writing about writing, they are forever quoting. Although overquoting is possible, most students of literature would improve their essays if they quoted more often than they do. A keen eye kept close to the text keeps the mind there, too, where the best ideas tend to hover. When quoting to give evidence, observe these three guidelines:

7.1.1 Support your debatable points only, not your undeniable ones. If discussing *Paradise Lost*, do not give a passage to establish that Eve is Adam's mate but do present relevant passages to develop the point that Milton presents his narrator as a heroic representative of fallen humanity.

7.1.2 Do not let the quoted writer's train of thought obstruct your own. Limit each quotation to your own point. For instance, if you are trying to show that in *The Subjection of Women* John Stuart Mill does not advocate identical roles for the two genders, do *not* quote him as follows: "The more rapid insight into character [. . .] [of] women over men, must certainly make them [. . .] more apt than men in [choosing fit administrators], which is nearly the most important business of everyone who has to do with governing mankind" (Mill 56). How much better to say instead, "Mill finds a 'more rapid insight into character' to be 'one of the admitted points of superiority of women over men'" (56). You will have kept to your point, sustained your pace, saved paper, and spared your reader.

7.1.3   In the same spirit, make all quotations as brief as possible and avoid overwhelming the reader with quotations, even if all help to prove your point. One or at most two quotations per moot point will probably do. If you still feel vulnerable, consider adding a few citations without quotation. For example, the scrupulous essayist on Mill might continue in parentheses, "See, too, 57-60, 64-66, and 84." All these references will assuage all but the doughtiest skepticism, yet they will not delay the reader ready to move on.

Essayists also quote to acknowledge borrowed ideas and to establish their place in an academic discussion. The good essay does not just repeat what has already been said. It builds on what has gone before, by clarifying previous discussion or by offering new grounds for agreement or disagreement. For instance, an essay might build on Aristotle's notion of mimesis or E. M. Forster's distinction between flat and round characters by applying the concept freshly and helpfully to a new literary work. Such an essay would quote the source of the concept or at least direct the reader to it by citing it. An essay would also acknowledge the source of any borrowed perception. It would even acknowledge sources that anticipate the essayist's original, self-generated ideas. A more ambitious essay might require citing several commentators to establish a prevailing climate of opinion or to document a difference of opinion.

Good essayists do not quote to argue from authority. Simply quoting a published opinion does not prove anything, because much that is published is wrong, and far more is debatable. Quotations and other citations can serve as the foundation of an essay but not as its keystone. Once the climate of opinion and the critical terms have been established, essayists must rely on their own logic, perceptiveness, and powers of persuasion. Of course, there is no harm in citing respected thinkers to point out that their observations support one's own line of thought.

7.1.4   If quoting to establish prevailing academic opinion, one should always be judicious, but one must be especially careful in citing electronic publications. Although printed academic books, as well as essays appearing in printed journals, are customarily reviewed by authorities in the field before they are accepted for publication, relatively few electronic publications receive such review, and many are self-published. Of course, many a vetted printed book or essay is woefully wrong-headed, some electronic publications are reviewed by authorities in the field, and some self-published electronic publications are perceptive, even authoritative. Therefore, exercise good judgment: value a good idea whatever its mode of publication but do not quote hole-and-corner sources as definitive.

In evaluating any publication, electronic or printed, consider many questions. What are the author's qualifications? Can they be verified? What is the purpose of the publication? What is its main point? How accurate is the information provided? How extensive is the author's knowledge of the field? Is the author's information and knowledge of relevant critical discussion up to date? What does the publication add to other publications on the same subject? Does the author deal with the topic and other commentary on it knowledgeably, intelligently, and fairly? The careful writer and thinker asks such questions of all secondary sources, but it is doubly important to ask them of electronic publications, because so few of them have undergone evaluation before publication.

7.2   Mechanics

7.2.1   **Quotation marks.** Quoted words are flanked by double quotation marks (" "). Use single quotation marks (' ') when quotation marks are needed in text already enclosed by quotation marks (see 4.11.4).

7.2.2   **Introductory punctuation.** (a) Ordinarily, when a quotation plays a role in the syntax of the writer's sentence, the quotation is introduced by a comma:

> John wailed, "Who ate all the Reduced-Fat Pecan Sandies?"

> Maud's dying words were, "The square of the hypotenuse is equal to the sum of the squares of the other two sides."

In the first example the quotation serves as direct object; in the second, as object complement. Although in every other situation a comma does not introduce direct objects or object complements, a comma does introduce them when they consist of a quotation.

When the quotation is brief—usually a word or phrase rather than a clause or complete sentence—the writer sometimes omits the introductory comma:

> No one yelled "Fire!"

> Sandy's tactless reply was "Arf!"

> The pale, puzzled faces brought to mind Hardy's "Dim moon-eyed fishes."

Also, the writer usually omits the introductory comma when the quotation serves as object of a preposition:

> The meaning of "What do you want of me?" is different from that of "What do you want of mine?"

(b) When a quotation does not serve a role in the syntax of the writer's sentence—when the syntax, although not necessarily the meaning, is complete without the quotation—a colon introduces the quotation. In 7.2.2 I have already insinuated two such colons in introducing examples. Often the writer will supply a helpful "as follows" or "the following" in leading up to the colon. Often, though, such a term is unnecessary, because the meaning is implied in the colon itself.

Sometimes, when the syntactically complete sentence leading up to the quotation is especially conclusive, the writer will use a period rather than a colon. The quotation follows without fanfare.

7.2.3 **Ellipses**. When quoting, mark an omission with a bracketed ellipsis. Here is a passage, followed by a quotation from it:

> As Apollo grasps the smooth, bare arm of Daphne, it turns rough to his touch. He embraces her and finds himself hugging bark. Her hair becomes leaves. Everything has changed except her shimmering grace.

> "[. . .] Daphne [. . .] turns rough to his touch. [. . .] Her hair becomes leaves."

See 4.5 for a more extensive treatment of the ellipsis.

7.2.4 **Brackets**. In addition to bracketing ellipses, bracket your words added to a quotation. If you capitalize the uncapitalized first word of a quotation, turning the quotation into a complete sentence, bracket your capital letter to show that you have done so:

> "[T]he smooth, bare arm of Daphne [. . .] turns rough to his [Apollo's] touch."

7.2.5 **Ending punctuation.** The most troublesome spot in a direct quotation is its ending, where the quotation mark must find its place among other marks of punctuation. This matter is discussed in 4.11.5. What follows repeats what is presented there:

> Place a period or comma inside the quotation marks. If, however, a parenthesis immediately follows the quotation, the period or comma follows the parenthesis.

Place a colon or semicolon outside the quotation marks.

Place a question mark or exclamation point inside or outside, on the basis of whether the mark punctuates the quoted matter or the larger sentence.

Whenever more than one of these six marks are called for at the end of a quotation, let a single mark stand for all. One period or comma will do for two, and one of the four larger marks will drive out a period or comma.

7.3   **Integration into text**

How writers fit a quotation into their own words depends on three factors: its form (prose versus poetry), its length, and the manner of acknowledging the source (a parenthetical reference versus a numbered note).

7.3.1   **Prose.** A prose quotation of roughly fifty words or more (five or more lines of typescript) is considered long; one of fewer words, short. Run a short quotation into the body of your text:

> Oliver Wendell Holmes reveals his genteel frame of mind in the playful but condescending observation that a "weak flavour of genius in an essentially common person is detestable," just as the "rinsings of an unwashed wineglass spoil a draught of fair water" (7).

Avoid long quotations if you can. If you must give one, set it off from the body of your text by indenting ten spaces from the left margin of your text:

> Swift's mockery multiplies. In the midst of ridiculing the unworldly impracticality of academicians, he has a professor propose a tax on those virtues on which men pride themselves:

> The highest Tax was upon Men who are the greatest Favourites of the other Sex, and the Assessments according to the Number and Natures of the Favours they have received; for which they are allowed to be their own Vouchers. Wit, Valour, and Politeness [i.e., suavity] were likewise proposed to be largely taxed, and collected in the same Manner, by every Person giving his own Word for the Quantum of what he possessed. But as to Honour, Justice, Wisdom and Learning, they should not be taxed at all; because, they are Qualifications of so singular a Kind, that no Man will either allow them in his Neighbour, or value them in himself. (152; pt. 3, ch. 6)

Here Swift mocks unworldliness and worldliness simultaneously.

Unless an indented quotation completes an introductory clause (as in "Swift's professor offers a ludicrous proposal, in which" followed without introductory punctuation by the indented quotation), introduce such a quotation by a colon or period. Do not put a long quotation into the middle of a clause, for by the end of the quotation readers will have lost their syntactic bearings. Do not set off an indented quotation with quotation marks: indentation is enough to show a quotation in progress. Double-space between the lines of the quotation and between the quotation and the body of your text.

7.3.2 **Poetry**. Except for a few modifications poetry is quoted in the same fashion as prose. More than three lines of poetry is considered a long quotation, to be indented. One line of poetry or less is always run into the body of the prose text:

> Anne Bradstreet's "But man was made for endless immortality" (1: 43) includes a triumphal tautology.

Treat a poetic quotation of intermediate length—more than one line but no more than three—in either way, as long as you are consistent throughout your text. When you run a few lines into the body of your text, indicate the end of a poetic line (unless it coincides with the end of your quoted passage) by a slash flanked by single spaces:

> William Hamilton of Bangour's "Where gat ye that bony bony bride? / Where gat ye that winsome marrow?" (649) may evoke visions of charnel love in readers unaware that *bony* here means "bonny" or "pretty," not "skeletal," and that *marrow* means "mate," not "the substance contained in the cavities of bones."

When you indent a passage of poetry, do not use the slash or quotation marks. Indent each line ten spaces from the left margin of your text (more, if the lines of poetry are short, to center the quotation) and also observe the poet's positioning of the lines in relation to one another:

> As I sat at the café, I said to myself,
> They may talk as they please about what they call pelf,
> They may sneer as they like about eating and drinking,
> But help it I cannot, I cannot help thinking
>   How pleasant it is to have money, heigh-ho!
>   How pleasant it is to have money.
>   (Clough 242)

The third factor determining the presentation of a quotation is, you will remember, the manner of directing the reader to information about the source of the quotation. The reader is directed to this information either by a parenthetical reference or by a note number. This chapter treats only the placement of the parenthetical reference or the note number in the body of the essay. The next two chapters, 8 and 9, discuss what to include in a parenthetical reference and how to present the information to which the parenthesis or note number refers. Chapter 8 shows how to compose a list of works cited; chapter 9 shows how to compose endnotes or footnotes.

7.3.3 Parenthetical References. For acknowledging sources, the Modern Language Association recommends parenthetical references to a list of works cited rather than superscript numeral references to notes. The recommendation, first made in 1984, marked a change in the standard scholarly format in the humanities—a change that promotes uniformity in scholarly notation by aligning the humanities with the physical and social sciences. So unless your teacher recommends otherwise, acknowledge your citations by means of parenthetical references to a list of works cited.

What goes into the parenthetical reference in the body of text is discussed at length in chapter 8. If you are discussing a single work, the parenthetical reference consists of just a page number or a line number. The first reference would include *page* or *line* in addition to the numeral. All later references would give just the numeral.

First reference:	(line 24)
Later references:	(43)

If you are citing more than one work, the reference consists of the last name of the cited work's author, followed without punctuation by a page- or line-number. Sometimes more information must be given and sometimes less, but the usual entry looks like this:

(Mill 56)

(Holmes 7)

The abbreviations *p.*, *pp.*, *l.*, and *ll.* are no longer recommended for acknowledging citations. Use just the numerals for page number(s) or line number(s).

In deciding where to place the parenthesis, weigh disruptiveness against unintelligibility: a parenthesis in mid-sentence may throw readers off stride, but one at the end of a paragraph may force them to double back in quest of the passage to which the parenthesis applies.

Unless you acknowledge more than one citation per parenthesis, be sure you give a parenthetical reference before moving on to your next citation. When you are quoting either prose or poetry run into the body of your text and the parenthesis follows immediately, the parenthesis follows all punctuation pertaining to the quotation, including the quotation marks, but precedes any punctuation pertaining to its place in the sentence as a whole.

> "[. . .] superiority of women over men" **(Mill 56).**

When a question mark or exclamation point of a quoted passage supplants a comma or the period of your own sentence (see 4.11.5.4 for the conditions under which this phenomenon takes place), put your comma or period after the parenthesis:

> In Faustus's speech in praise of Helen, "Was this the face that launched a thousand ships / And burnt the topless towers of Ilium?" (Marlowe 5.1.98-99)**,** Faustus praises Helen more for her power than for her beauty.

> Faustus praises Helen: "Was this the face that launched a thousand ships / And burnt the topless towers of Ilium?" (Marlowe 5.1.98-99)**.** Characteristically, he praises her more for her power than for her beauty.

When indenting a prose quotation, punctuate the end of the quotation as though there were no parenthesis following it. Then skip two spaces after the end punctuation and give the parenthetical reference with no punctuation before or after the parenthesis:

> The highest Tax was upon Men who are the greatest Favourites of the other Sex, and the Assessments according to the Number and Natures of the Favours they have received; for which they are allowed to be their own Vouchers. Wit, Valour, and Politeness were likewise proposed to be largely

taxed, and collected in the same Manner, by every
Person giving his own Word for the Quantum of
what he possessed. But as to Honour, Justice,
Wisdom and Learning, they should not be taxed at
all; because, they are Qualifications of so singular
a Kind, that no Man will either allow them in his
Neighbour, or value them in himself. **(Swift 152)**

When indenting a passage of poetry, punctuate the poetry as though there were no parenthesis. Then skip to
the next line after the last line of poetry and place the parenthesis flush with the right margin of the quotation.
Do not put a period after the parenthesis.

> There will I build him
> A monument, and plant it round with shade
> Of laurel ever green and branching palm,
> With all his trophies hung, and acts enrolled
> In copious legend, or sweet lyric song.
> Thither shall all the valiant youth resort,
> And from his memory inflame their breasts
> To matchless valor and adventures high.
> (Milton 1733-40)

Either your text or your entry in the list of works cited
would inform the reader that the poem being quoted is
Samson Agonistes.

7.3.4 Numbered-Note References. The traditional means of
acknowledging one's sources—notes—is being sup-
planted by parenthetical reference to a list of works
cited. But because many writers, teachers, and editors
still prefer notes, because you will read many works that
use notes, and because even those works using parenthetical reference will also use notes for some purposes,
I discuss here how to use note-numbers. In chapter 9 I
discuss how to compose the bibliographical notes to
which the numbers refer.

In numbered-note reference, almost all *first* references to a text are identified in numbered notes. Occasionally, when there are only a few texts cited, the texts will be identified in a lengthy parenthesis (see, for example, the references to Harding and Auden in chapter 6). But for a first reference a note is usually better because less disruptive of your prose. This chapter has already used six parenthetical references. If we were using the numbered-note system, the text would have looked like this:

> "[. . .] the most important business of everyone who has to do with governing mankind."[1] How much better to say instead [. . .].

> "[A] weak flavour of genius in an essentially common person is detestable," just as the "rinsings of an unwashed wineglass spoil a draught of fair water."[2]

> [T]hey are Qualifications of so singular a Kind, that no Man will either allow them in his Neighbour, or value them in himself.[3]

> Anne Bradstreet's "But man was made for endless immortality" includes a triumphal tautology.[4]

> "Where gat ye that bony bony bride? / Where gat ye that winsome marrow?"[5]

> How pleasant it is to have money, heigh-ho! How pleasant it is to have money.[6]

The note number comes immediately after the quotation or after the sentence or paragraph of which the quotation is a part. The note number follows all punctuation (except a dash) trailing the word after which the number is to appear. Thus the note number follows a period, quotation marks, and parentheses. The number follows immediately, with no intervening space. It has no period after it or parentheses around it. It is raised higher than the other text on its line.

In the numbered-note system, the second note and all later notes referring to a given work are less extensive than the first one. To make such subsequent acknowledgments, you can use note numbers and notes. But if you cite a text frequently, you can often do so with least trouble to you and your reader by using brief parentheses within your text to acknowledge all citations after the first one. Where there is no ambiguity as to what work you are citing, a parenthetical page number or line number is all you need give.

Works Cited in Chapter 7

Bradstreet, Anne. "Contemplations." The American Tradition in Literature. Ed. Sculley Bradley et al. 4th ed. 2 vols. New York: Norton, 1974. 39-45.

Clough, Arthur Hugh. Dipsychus. The Poems. Ed. A. L. P. Norrington. London: Oxford UP, 1968. 221-96.

Hamilton, William, of Bangour. "The Braes of Yarrow [. . .] in Imitation of the Ancient Scottish Manner." A Collection of English Poems: 1660-1800. Ed. Ronald S. Crane. New York: Harper, 1932. 648-52.

Holmes, Oliver Wendell. The Autocrat of the Breakfast Table. London: Everyman-Dent, 1906.

Mill, John Stuart. The Subjection of Women. Cambridge, MA: MIT UP, 1970.

Swift, Jonathan. Gulliver's Travels. Gulliver's Travels and Other Writings. 1726. New York: Modern Library-Random, 1958. 1-243.

Notes to Chapter 7

[1] The Subjection of Women (Cambridge, MA: MIT UP, 1970) 56.

[2] The Autocrat of the Breakfast Table (London: Everyman-Dent, 1906) 7.

[3] Jonathan Swift, Gulliver's Travels, in Gulliver's Travels and Other Writings (New York: Modern Library-Random, 2958) 152.

[4] "Contemplations," The American Tradition in Literature, ed. Sculley Bradley et al., 4th ed., 2 vols. (New York: Norton, 1974) 1: 43.

[5] "The Braes of Yarrow [. . .] in Imitation of the Ancient Scottish Manner," A Collection of English Poems: 1660-1800, ed. Ronald S. Crane (New York: Harper, 1932) 649.

[6] Arthur Hugh Clough, Dipsychus, in The Poems, ed. A. L. P. Norrington (London: Oxford UP, 1968) 242; 4.130-35.

8. Reference to a List of Works Cited

To acknowledge works cited, one follows a host of conventions. Observing the conventions is a fussy business. But they do enable one to give enormous quantities of information systematically, precisely, compactly, and unobtrusively. Using the conventions is a courtesy to the reader and an exercise in concision.

Before 1984 the humanities acknowledged sources by means of footnotes or endnotes; the social and physical sciences, by means of parenthetical references to a list of works cited. But in 1984 the Modern Language Association of America, the largest professional organization of scholars in the humanities, endorsed what is essentially the notation system of the sciences. The recommendations of the MLA are detailed in Joseph Gibaldi, MLA Handbook for Writers of Research Papers, 4th ed., New York: MLA, 1995, and, more recently, in Gibaldi, MLA Style Manual and Guide to Scholarly Publishing, 2nd ed., New York: MLA, 1998. This chapter is an abridged account of these recommendations. To acknowledge a work beyond the scope of this chapter, see the MLA Handbook. An alternative, Michael Meyer, The Little, Brown Guide to Writing Research Papers, 3d ed., Boston: Little, 1994, gives the same information in a good, readable format and leads the student through the whole process of writing a research paper. The university's bookstore stocks all three books.

Although the MLA's system of acknowledging citations is now much closer than it was to that of other scholarly fields, some fields have a slightly different set of conventions. Section 8.3

mentions some variations and lists the style manuals of several other academic fields.

Some teachers continue to prefer numbered notes for acknowledging citations, and many academic and general publications still use notes. Furthermore, even the MLA system recommends notes for a multiple reference or for non-bibliographical information. Notes are treated in the next chapter.

If you are writing a paper for an English course, use the conventions described in this chapter, unless your teacher tells you to use different ones. Ask your teachers in other departments what conventions they wish you to use in papers written for them.

Giving all the rules for acknowledging citations would turn this booklet into a tome. This chapter presents only the basic rules and then gives various examples. The examples probably cover almost all the kinds of texts you will be acknowledging. Carefully match each of your bibliographical entries with the appropriate example.

8.1 General Rules

A list of works cited is given at the end of the essay or chapter. The list is arranged alphabetically according to the author's last name.

The works listed are referred to in the body of the text by means of parenthetical entries. See 7.3.3 for where to place the parentheses and how to punctuate them.

8.1.1 The parenthetical reference.

8.1.1.1 The simplest parenthetical reference occurs when the list of cited works consists of a single entry. The situation arises in literature courses when the student discusses without reference to secondary sources a single poem, short story, play, novel, or essay. In this situation, if using an assigned edition of a short story, novel, or essay, give only the page or line number(s) in your parenthetical reference. The first reference should give *line* or *page* along with the numeral; later references should give the line number or page number only:

> **First reference:** "How easy 'tis for parents to forgive" (line 386).

> **Second reference:** "But he, though bad, is followed by a worse" (583).

If you are discussing a very short poem, in which your reader can easily locate your quotation, no reference is necessary.

If discussing a play divided into numbered acts, scenes, and lines, refer in parentheses to the act, scene, and line rather than to the page:

> "This my hand will rather / The multitudinous seas incarnadine, / Making the green one red" (2.2.60-63).

If the topic of your essay requires you to range beyond literary works included in textbooks assigned in the course, you may, as an act of courtesy to your reader, add to the standard, required page reference a reference appropriate to the genre. Separate the two references by a semicolon:

> When Silas returns to Lantern Yard, he finds the little chapel transformed into a large factory (163; ch. 21).

But if there is an assigned edition of a short story, novel, or essay and you read the work in a different edition, borrow a copy of the assigned edition to make your references conform to it.

8.1.1.2 When the list of works cited consists of more than one work, the basic reference consists of a last name and a page number or line number. There is no comma between name and number:

> Piggy squints through his broken spectacles (Golding 191).

8.1.1.3 The purpose of the reference is, if course, to direct the reader to a specific passage within a specific work. If the purpose can be accomplished more briefly, do so. If, for example, you mention the author's name in your passage, the name need not be included in the parenthetical reference:

> Golding stresses Piggy's struggles to see through the broken spectacles (191).

If discussing an electronically published work without page numbers, give in parentheses any available information to help your reader find it.

8.1.1.4 If the cited work does not give the name of its author, the title or a shortened title serves in place of the author's name. If a shortened title is used, it should begin with the word by which the title is alphabetized in the list of works cited.

> Codfish Falls Road of Mansfield, Connecticut, was formerly Clarktown Road (Annual Report 121).

8.1.1.5 If the title of a work should be given in quotation marks rather than italics (see 5.3.5), it should be so given in a parenthetical reference:

> In 1920 the University of Connecticut enrollment for the spring semester was 354 regular students and 1 graduate student ("Report of Town Clerk" 26).

8.1.1.6 A parenthetical reference may require additional information. If, for instance, more than one work by William Golding is under discussion, the title or a shortened title should be included along with his name and the page number. If a shortened title is used, it should begin with the word by which the title is alphabetized in the list of works cited:

> Piggy blinks behind his broken spectacles (Golding, Lord 191).

Lord here indicates *Lord of the Flies*. There is a comma between name and title, none between title and page number.

8.1.1.7 If the cited work consists of more than one volume, give the appropriate volume number. The number, followed by a colon and a space, precedes the page number:

> The Crimean War "exhibited the soundness of the British regimental drill and tradition, and the utter incompetence of the higher command [. . .]" (Trevelyan 3: 198).

8.1.1.8 If the reference is to an entire volume, not to a specific passage, the parenthetical reference would look like this:

> According to one historian, the most important changes in England during the past three centuries have been the advent of the industrial revolution and the transition to democracy (Trevelyan, vol. 3).

In this reference there is a comma after the author's name, and there is no colon. Although a colon signifies that the numeral preceding it is a volume number, a colon also signifies that something follows. Here, because there is no page number to follow the colon, *vol.* is used instead of a colon.

8.1.1.9 If the list of works cited includes two or more sole authors with the same last name, the parenthetical reference should include the cited author's first name(s). If, for instance, an essay includes citations of Dante Gabriel Rossetti and Christina Rossetti, an essayist would acknowledge a citation as follows:

> The confused self-questioning of the Victorians is revealed in the clutter of mirrors in the poetry: "All my walls are lost in mirrors, whereupon I trace / Self to right hand, self to left hand, self in every place, / Self-same solitary figure, self-same seeking face" (Christina Rossetti 149).

The entry implies that only one work by Christina Rossetti is cited in the essayist's work. If more than one work is cited, then each is acknowledged in the list of works cited, and the parenthetical reference would look like this:

> (Christina Rossetti, "Royal Princess" 149).

8.1.1.10 If a work has two or three authors, courtesy prevails over brevity: the parenthetical reference gives all the last names, in the order in which the title page presents them. But courtesy has its limit: if a work has more than three authors, the parenthetical reference gives the last name of the first author only, followed by *et al.* (the Latin abbreviation for *et alii*, "and others"):

> Thomas Sturge Moore "outlived his reputation and wrote too much" (Wiley and Orel 340).

> In the sixteenth century spelling was unstable: "[A] man varied the spelling of even his name to suit convenience or a whim" (Abrams et al. 1: 510).

8.1.2 The list of works cited

Start the list on a new page after the final page of the text. If the essay contains endnotes in addition to a list of works cited, start the list on a new page after the final note. Paginate consecutively throughout the essay, notes, and list. Center the title, "Works Cited," one inch from the top of the sheet (do not enclose your title in quotation marks). Double-space between lines throughout the list: within each entry and between entries.

Include in the list *all* works cited in the text and *only* those works. Arrange entries alphabetically according to author's last name, or, if the author's name is not given, according to work's title. Do not indent the first line of the entry. Indent each subsequent line of the entry five spaces.

8.1.2.1 Books.

Most book entries consist of three items: the author's name, the work's title, and publishing information. But an entry may consist of as many as nine items. Each item begins with a capital letter and ends with a period, followed by two spaces. Items are given in the following order:

1.   Author's name

2.   Title of cited work within the larger work

3.   Title of larger work

4.   Editor's or translator's name

5.   Edition

6.   Number of volumes

7.   Name of the series

8.   City of publication, publisher, and date of publication

9.   Page numbers of cited work within the larger work

> Nimoy, Leonard. "Food for Thought." <u>Out of This World: Favorite Recipes of Famous Extraterrestrials</u>. Ed. Sally Ride. 4th ed. 2 vols. <u>Better Living through Astronomy Series</u> 12. Dallas, TX: Galaxy, 1999. 2: 429-32.

Author's name. Give the last name of the author before the first name. If there is more than one author, reverse the names of the first author only. Do not omit any part of an author's name as it is given on the work's title page. You may but need not complete in brackets names given as initials. You may but need not add in brackets the name of an author using a pen name.

Title of work. Type a line under the entire title, including subtitle and punctuation within the title. Do not underline the period that ends this item. If the title mentions a title that would also ordinarily take underlining, do not underline the title within the title.

Number of volumes. Give the total number of volumes of a several-volume work, even if you cite only one volume of the work.

City of publication, publisher, and date. If the title-page gives more than one city as the city of publication, give only the first-mentioned city. If the city's name is ambiguous or might be unfamiliar to the reader, add a standard abbreviation for the state or country of publication. After the name of the city (and state or country), put a colon, followed by a single space.

Use a standard abbreviation for publisher's name. For most publishers the abbreviation is the first proper name of the title. But if the name of the press includes "University Press," its abbreviation, *UP*, is always included in citing the press. For a list of abbreviations see *MLA Handbook* 218-20 or Meyer. If no publisher is named on the title page, put *n.p.* (no publisher) in place of a name. After the name of publisher (or *n.p.*) put a comma, followed by a single space.

Thereafter put the year of publication. Most books give this information on the title page. If the date is not given there, look for it on the copyright page, which follows. If no date of publication is given on either page, give the latest copyright date. Be sure that the date you give is the date of publication of the latest *edition*, not just the date of the latest printing or impression. If these pages yield no year of publication, put *n.d.* (no date) instead.

Page numbers of cited work. Give page numbers if the text you cite is included in a larger work, such as an anthology. Give the page numbers for the entire text cited, not for just the cited portion of the text. If the larger work consists of more than one volume, include the appropriate volume number in the pagination.

8.1.2.2 Articles in periodicals.

The entry for an article consists of three parts: name of author, title of article, and publication information. Each part ends with a period followed by two spaces. The publication information consists of the name of the periodical, the number or name of the series, the volume number, the year of publication, and the page numbers of the article.

1.   Author's name

2.   Title of cited article

3.   Publication information

    a.   Name of periodical

    b.   Number or name of series

    c.   Volume number

    d.   Year of publication

    e.   Page numbers of article

       Murphy, James J. "A New Look at Chaucer and the Rhetoricians." <u>Review of English Studies</u> ns 15 (1964): 1-20.

Title of cited article. Enclose the title in quotation marks. The period at the end of the item goes before the closing quotation mark.

Name of periodical. Omit any introductory *a*, *an*, or *the*. Otherwise, give the name as it appears on the title page of the periodical. Do not abbreviate. Underline the name, including spaces and punctuation between words. Do not punctuate immediately after the name.

Number or name of series. A few periodicals have changed their series, beginning anew with volume number 1. After the name of such a periodical, give the appropriate abbreviation for the series: for instance, *ns* ("new series"), *os* ("old series"), *4th ser.* ("fourth series"). Begin the abbreviation one space after the name of the periodical, with no intervening punctuation. Except for the period of *ser.*, do not punctuate immediately after the number or name of the series.

Volume number. A typical scholarly periodical publishes four issues per year. After the year's issues have been published, they are bound into a single, numbered volume. An acknowledgment of an article includes the periodical's volume number, which directs a reader to the appropriate volume within the series on the library's shelf. Give the volume number in Arabic numerals. If the periodical is paginated consecutively throughout all issues of a volume, give just the volume number. If the periodical begins each issue with page 1, give the issue number immediately after the volume number and a decimal point. For example, the volume number of the third issue of the tenth volume of a periodical so paginated would be given as *10.3*. The issue number in the bibliographical entry signifies that pagination is not consecutive throughout the volume. See 8.2.11 and 8.2.12 for further refinements. Do not punctuate immediately after the volume number.

Year of publication. Enclose this entry in parentheses. Thereafter put a colon and a single space.

Page numbers of article. Give the page numbers for the entire article cited, not for just the cited portion of the article. If the article is interrupted by pages of other printed matter, give the article's first page number and then, with no intervening space, a plus sign. Put a period after the page numbers.

8.1.2.3 Electronic Publications

Let me repeat what is said in the previous chapter: if quoting to establish prevailing academic opinion, be judicious in citing electronic publications. Although printed academic books, as well as essays appearing in printed journals, are customarily reviewed by authorities in the field before they are accepted for publication, relatively few electronic publications receive such review, and many are self-published. Of course, many a vetted printed book or essay is woefully wrong-headed, some electronic publications are reviewed by authorities in the field, and some self-published electronic publications are perceptive, even authoritative. Therefore, be judicious: value a good idea whatever its mode of publication but do not quote hole-and-corner sources as definitive. See 7.1.4 for questions to consider in evaluating a secondary source, electronic or printed.

Two problems arise in citing online publications: volatile, even vanishing texts and, in many works, no page numbers. To minimize the first problem, include at least two dates in your citation of online texts: the date given in the source and that on which you consulted the publication. Also, it is a good idea to download or print out at the time you consult the publication sections especially important to your own work. You or your teacher can then easily refer to them thereafter. To minimize the absence of page numbers in an electronic publication that lacks them, give whatever information you can (e.g., paragraph numbers) that helps your reader locate the citation.

The key element in citing any online publication is its network address, also known as its uniform resource locator (URL).

<http://www.coolrunning.com/
results/97/ct/hart1018.htm>

Give the complete address, including the access-mode identifier (*http, ftp, gopher, telnet, news*). In your list entry enclose the URL in angle brackets. Some addresses are very long. If an address overruns a line, divide the address after a slash only and take the necessary measures to keep your word-processing program from hyphenating at the break.

An electronically published book. Insofar as it is possible to do so, the citation for an electronic publication mirrors that for its printed counterpart. For example, the citation for an electronically published book lists relevant items in the order given in 8.1.2.1 and in the format recommended there: author's name, title of cited work within the larger work, title of larger work, editor's or translator's name, edition, number of volumes, name of series, and publication information. Immediately after giving all such information that is relevant and can be found and ending with the date of publication and a period, the citation for an electronically published book double spaces and then gives the date on which the book was consulted. After another double space the citation gives the book's full network address, enclosed in angle brackets. The citation ends with a period.

An electronically published essay. Similarly, the citation for an electronically published essay lists relevant items in the order given in 8.1.2.2 and in the format recommended there: author's name, title of cited article, name of periodical, number or name of series, volume number, year of publication. Immediately after giving all such information that is relevant and can be found and ending with the date of publication and a period, the citation for an electronically published essay double spaces and then gives the date on which the essay was consulted. After another double space the citation gives the essay's full network address, enclosed in angle brackets. The citation ends with a period.

A personal Web site. Begin with the name of the author of the site, giving surname first. Next give the title of the site, capitalizing and underlining as you would the title of a book. If the site has no title, give a generic description, such as *Home page*, without italics or underlining. Then give the name of any organization associated with the site and the date on which the site was last revised (if the date is given). If the site is unrevised, give the date it was created. Finally, give the date you consulted the site and the electronic address. Enclose the electronic address in angle brackets. Double space between entries. Put a period after all entries except the date of accessing the site.

A nonperiodical publication on CD-ROM, diskette, or magnetic tape. Because a publication on CD-ROM, diskette, or magnetic tape is stabler than its ethereal counterparts, it is not necessary to give the date such a work is consulted. Again the citation follows that for a printed work. Immediately before giving information pertaining to the electronic publication (city, publisher, date), mention the medium of publication (e.g., "CD-ROM"), followed by a period. If the CD-ROM reproduces an already-published text, give publication information both for the original publisher and for the subsequent vendor.

> Dickens, Charles. <u>A Christmas Carol</u>. London: Longman, 1991. CD-ROM. Foster City, CA: DynEd, 1994.

A work from a periodically published database on CD-ROM. Begin by providing all bibliographical data on the work in its original, printed form. Then give the title, underlined, of the database (e.g., <u>ERIC</u>, <u>Sociofile</u>, <u>Dissertation Abstracts Ondisc</u>, <u>Congressional Masterfile</u>), followed by a period. Mention the publication medium (e.g., CD-ROM), followed by a period. Give the vendor's name, followed by a period. Finally, give the electronic publication date, followed by a period.

8.2 Examples of List Entries

The style of your list entries should be the same as that of those given here, except that your entries should be in alphabetical order and the lines of your entries should be double-spaced.

8.2.1 A book with one author:

Chesser, Eustace. <u>Salvation Through Sex: The Life and Work of Wilhelm Reich</u>. New York: Morrow, 1972.

Headlee, Thomas J. <u>The Mosquitoes of New Jersey and Their Control</u>. New Brunswick, NJ: Rutgers UP, 1945.

Morrow stands for "William Morrow." Because universities issue publications in addition to those issued by university presses, include *UP* wherever it applies, to avoid ambiguity. Other presses can usually be cited in briefer form.

8.2.2 A book with more than one author:

<u>The Norton Anthology of Poetry</u>. Ed. Arthur M. Eastman et al. New York: Norton, 1970.

Raistrick, Arthur, and Bernard Jennings. <u>A History of Lead Mining in the Pennines</u>. London: Longman, 1965.

As here, list authors in the order given on the title page, not in alphabetical order according to last name. When a work has two or three authors (or editors), mention them all. When a work has more than three authors (or editors), use the abbreviation *et al.*, meaning "and others," after giving the first-named author (or editor).

8.2.3   An edition:

> Gliner, Robert, and R. A. Raines, ed. <u>Munching on Existence: Contemporary American Society through Literature</u>. New York: Free, 1971.

> Kingsmill, Hugh, [Lunn], ed. <u>An Anthology of Invective and Abuse</u>. New York: Dial, 1929.

> <u>An Anthology of Invective and Abuse</u>. Ed. Hugh Kingsmill [Lunn]. New York: Dial, 1929.

If the author of the work is not known or if the work is an anthology, the first item of the entry would be either the title of the work or the name of the editor. The choice would depend on which term is more important to your essay.

If, as here, you supply information not given in the text, enclose it in brackets. In the Kingsmill entry brackets enclose the surname of the author, who chooses to publish under a pseudonym. In 8.2.8 brackets are used in giving the author's name in full whereas the text gives only initials plus surname.

> Lavater, Ludwig. <u>Of Ghostes and Spirites Walking by Nyght</u>. Ed. J. Dover Wilson and May Yardley. Oxford: Oxford UP, 1929.

> Wilson, J. Dover, and May Yardley, ed. <u>Of Ghostes and Spirites Walking by Nyght</u>. By Ludwig Lavater. Oxford: Oxford UP, 1929.

If the name of an editor appears on the title page, give the name in your entry. If the author of the work is known, the author's name is almost always given as the first item of the entry (for example, "Lavater, Ludwig . . ."). If, as occasionally happens, your essay focuses on the editor rather than the author, give the editor's name as the first item of the entry (for example, "Wilson, J. Dover . . .").

8.2.4   The standard edition of an author's works:

> Clough, Arthur Hugh. <u>The Poems of Arthur Hugh Clough</u>. Ed. A. L. P. Norrington. London: Oxford UP, 1968.

> Clough, Arthur Hugh. <u>The Poems</u>. Ed. A. L. P. Norrington. London: Oxford UP, 1968.

Either form is proper. The second saves space by mentioning the poet's name but once.

8.2.5   A second or later edition:

> Brooks, Cleanth, and Robert Penn Warren. <u>Understanding Poetry</u>. 4th ed. New York: Holt, 1976.

A list entry mentions the year in which the *edition* of the cited book was first published. The conventions of notation do not require you to mention the year of publication of any other edition of the book. If, though, such a date is relevant to your essay, then add it. For example, if you were discussing Brooks and Warren's influential book, you might add to your note, "First pub. 1938."

8.2.6   A book reprinted by a second publisher:

> Orwell, George. <u>1984.</u> 1949. Rpt. New York: Signet-NAL, 1961.

Reprinting a book involves reusing plates of type already set for an earlier printing; producing a new edition involves setting type anew. When you cite a work reprinted by the original publisher, give the first year of publication of the edition, not the year of the reprinting. But if citing a work reprinted by a publisher other than the original one, follow the pattern of the example given here. It does not note the original publisher of the edition, but it does note the first year of publication of the edition, the publisher of the reprinted book, and the first year of the reprinting by the second publisher. Reprinting by a second publisher is not so rare as one might suppose. A publisher of paperbacks often makes arrangements with the publisher of a hardcover book to reuse type already set for the hardcover book. Such information is to be found on a book's title page and copyright page. If, as is often true of paperbacks, the book is published under a publisher's special imprint, follow the present example in giving imprint name, then publisher's name, with one unspaced hyphen between the names.

Read the copyright page carefully to determine the category of the book you are citing. Not all paperback books are reprints of an earlier publication. Some are fresh editions of a previously published work; some are original publications. The chapter has already provided examples of notation for the latter categories.

8.2.7   A translation:

> Jalovec, Karol. <u>Beautiful Italian Violins</u>. Trans. J. B. Kozác. London: Hamlyn, 1963.

8.2.8   A work of more than one volume:

> Bates, E. Stuart. <u>Inside Out: An Introduction to Autobiography</u>. 2 vols. Oxford: Blackwell, 1935-37.

> Doyle, Arthur Conan.   "The Adventure of the Blanched Soldier." <u>The Complete Sherlock Holmes</u>. 2 vols. Garden City, NJ: Doubleday, n.d. 2: 1000-12.

> <u>A Selection of African Prose</u>. Comp. W[ilfred] H[owell] Whitely. 2 vols. Oxford: Clarendon, 1964.

8.2.9   A play or long poem:

> <u>Gammer Gurtons Nedle</u>. <u>Chief Pre-Shakespearean Dramas</u>. Ed. Joseph Quincy Adams. Cambridge, MA: Riverside, 1924. 469-99.

8.2.10 A shorter poem:

> Carew, Thomas. "A Rapture." <u>Norton Anthology of English Literature</u>. Ed. M. H. Abrams et al. 4th ed. 2 vols. New York: Norton, 1979. 1: 1596-1600.

> Stevens, Wallace. "The River of Rivers in Connecticut." <u>Collected Poems</u>. New York: Knopf, 1957. 533.

8.2.11 An article in a periodical:

> Ruston, A. F. "A Note on Clorms." <u>London Mathematical Society Journal</u> 32 (1957): 110-12.

> Hill, R. D. "Pepper Growing in Johore." <u>Journal of Tropical Geography</u> 28.3 (1969): 30-42.

Dreikurs, Rudolph. "The Choice of a Mate." <u>International Journal of Individual Psychology</u> 1.4 (1935): 99-102.

Flygers, Vagn. "Hunters of White Whales." <u>The Beaver</u> Winter 1965: 35.

The Ruston entry refers to an article in a periodical that paginates consecutively throughout all issues of a volume. The Hill and Dreikurs entries refer to articles in periodicals that collect issues into volumes but begin each issue with page *1*. The Flygers entry refers to an article in a periodical that does not publish in volumes. When listing an article published in such a periodical, give the date of the issue instead of volume number followed (in parentheses) by year.

8.2.12 A newspaper or weekly or monthly magazine:

"Mick Jagger Comments on Margaret Trudeau." <u>Chicago Tribune</u> 15 Sept. 1977, city ed., sec. 1: 5.

Lescelles, Gerald. "The Chase of the Wild Fallow Deer." <u>Nineteenth Century</u> Oct. 1886: 509-10.

Underline the title of the newspaper. The name of the city in which the newspaper is published may or may not be part of the newspaper's title. The name plate of the newspaper, displayed at the top of the first page, includes the name of the city if the name is part of the newspaper's title.

In works not published in volumes, the date of the issue serves instead of volume number and year. Abbreviate all months except *May, June,* and *July.*

Specify the newspaper's edition—for example, city edition, late edition, national edition, Sunday edition—if the edition is given on the name plate. Unless the paper is paginated consecutively throughout, specify the section as well. If sections are lettered, a page-reference might be B4.

8.2.13 A review:

> Romanucci-Ross, Lola. "The Old Lamplighters and the Case of the Curious Episteme: Fox and Freud and the Nature of Primatology." Rev. of The Red Lamp of Incest, by Robin Fox. Reviews in Anthropology 8 (1981): 443.

> Wolff, Leanne O. Rev. of Presidential Rhetoric: 1961-1980, ed. Theodore Windt. Presidential Studies Quarterly 9 (1981): 589-90.

> "What to Feel Where." Rev. of Abroad: A Book of Travels, ed. Jon Evans. Times Literary Supplement 16 Jan. 1969: 59.

Reviews may be signed or unsigned, titled or untitled. Follow the pattern of the appropriate example.

8.2.14 A work in an anthology:

> Wright, Richard. "Big Boy Leaves Home." An Introduction to Literature. Ed. William Chace and Peter Collier. San Diego: Harcourt, 1985. 149-76.

8.2.15 An electronically published book:

> Ruskin, John. The King of the Golden River. Champagne, IL: Project Gutenberg, 1996. 4 June 1998 <ftp//uiarchive.cso.uiuc.edu/ pub/etext/gutenberg/etext96/ tkogr10.txt>.

8.2.16 An article in an electronically published periodical:

> Lancashire, Ian. "The Common Reader's Shake-
>   speare." <u>Early Modern Literary Studies</u>
>   3.3 Special Issue 2 (Jan. 1998): 4.1-12. 5
>   June 1998
>   <http://www.humanities.ualberta.ca/
>   emls/03-3/lancshak.html>.

This periodical is not paginated, but for easy reference it
numbers its essays as well as the paragraphs of each essay. The "4.1-12" indicates that the essay is the fourth essay if the issue and that the essay comprises twelve
paragraphs.

8.2.17 A personal Web site:

> Salomon, David A. <u>Hamlet in Hyperspace</u>. Uni-
>   versity of Connecticut. 3 March 1998. 5
>   June 1998 <http://www.sp.uconn.edu/
>   ~das93006/429/ home.html>.

8.2.18 A nonperiodical publication on CD-ROM:

> "Meerschaum." <u>Oxford English Dictionary</u>. 2nd
>   ed. CD-ROM. Oxford: Oxford UP, 1992.

> Dickens, Charles. <u>A Christmas Carol</u>. London:
>   Longman, 1991. CD-ROM. Foster City,
>   CA: DynEd, 1994.

The second entry is more extensive because the cited
work is an exact reproduction of a printed one. The first
entry is not.

8.2.19 A work from a periodically published database on CD-ROM:

> Loy, Pamela Stephanie. "Victoria's Camelot:
>   Love, Work, and the Arthurian Revival."
>   <u>DAI</u> 58 (1997): 3145A. U of Georgia,
>   1997. <u>Dissertation Abstracts Ondisc</u>.
>   CD-ROM. UMI-Proquest. Dec. 1997.

8.3 | **Other Reference Systems**

Although almost all academic fields now acknowledge citations by means of parenthetical references to a list of works cited, there are differences from field to field. This section merely touches on three additional reference systems: author-title, author-date, and numeral.

8.3.1 Author-title system

This system is common in the physical sciences. In the first reference to a work give the last name(s) of the author(s) and a distinguishing word from the title: (Headlee, Mosquitoes). If citing two or more authors with the same surname, include the initials of their given names. If referring to only a part of a work, cite the relevant page or pages: (Headlee, Mosquitoes: 22-23). If a work has more than two authors, in second and later references give the surname of the first author only, followed by "et al." If the practice would produce ambiguity, cite all authors. The list of works cited follows this form:

Dreikurs, R. The choice of a mate. International Journal of Individual Psychology, 1935, 1(4), 99-102.

Holloway, J. Logic, feeling, & structure in political oratory: a primer of analysis. In G. Levine & W. Madden (Eds.), The art of Victorian prose. New York: Oxford UP, 1968.

Raistrick, A., & Jennings, B. A history of lead mining in the Pennines. London: Longman, 1965.

Ruston, A. F. A note on clorms. London Mathematical Society Journal, 1957, 32, 110-12.

There are several differences from the MLA style:

- No first names are given.

- The surname is given first for all authors, not just the first-named one.

- In the title of the work, only the first word and proper nouns are capitalized.

- The ampersand (&) is always used in place of *and*.

- The date precedes the volume number of a journal.

- The volume number is italicized (underlined).

- No quotation marks are used.

8.3.2   Author-date system

Within the text proceed as in 8.3.1, substituting the date of the publication for its short title: (Hill 1969: 42). If you cite more than one article published by an author in a given year, add to the date a different lower-case letter for each article published in the year (Hill 1969b: 42). In the list of works cited give the date of the publication immediately after the name of the author(s).

> Hill, R. D. 1969. "Pepper Growing in Johore."
> Journal of Tropical Geography 28.3: 30-42.

8.3.3   Numeral system

Number all entries in the reference list. The entries are in alphabetical order, according to the surname of each author (or, in the case of multiple authors, first author) cited.

> 1. Dreikurs, R. . . .
>
> 2. Holloway, J. . . .

> In the text cite parenthetically only the numeral of the entry. In some versions of the system the numeral is underlined; in others, not. Add page numbers, too, where they apply: (35, 345-49).

For detailed information on the recommended format for essays in a given academic field, consult a teacher in that field or read a style manual for that field. The following list of such manuals is reprinted from the <u>MLA Style Manual and Guide to Scholarly Publishing</u>, with the permission of the Modern Language Association of America. Copyright 1985, 1998 by MLA:

Biology

Council of Biology Editors. Style Manual Committee. <u>CBE Style Manual: A Guide for Authors, Editors, and Publishers in the Biological Sciences</u>. 6th ed. Bethesda: Council of Biology Editors, 1994.

Chemistry

American Chemical Society. <u>The ACS Style Guide: A Manual for Authors and Editors</u>. Washington: American Chemical Soc., 1986.

Geology

United States. Geological Survey. <u>Suggestions to Authors of the Reports of the United States Geological Survey</u>. 7th ed. Washington: GPO, 1991.

Linguistics

Linguistic Society of America. <u>LSA Bulletin</u>, Dec. issue, annually.

Mathematics

American Mathematical Society. <u>A Manual for Authors of Mathematical Papers</u>. 8th ed. Providence: American Mathematical Soc., 1990.

Medicine

American Medical Association. <u>AMA Manual of Style</u>. 8th ed.
        Chicago: Amer. Medical Assn., 1990.

Physics

American Institute of Physics. <u>Style Manual for Guidance in the
        Preparation of Papers</u>. 4th ed. New York: American Inst.
        of Physics, 1990.

Psychology

American Psychological Association. <u>Publication Manual of the
        American Psychological Association</u>. 4th ed.
        Washington: American Psychological Assn., 1994.

The following two pages illustrate the MLA system of parenthetical references to a list of works cited:

Meortsnos 2

Grandet is unique among the misers of literature. Most are materialistic visionaries, filled with vivid dreams of "infinite riches in a little room" (Marlowe 201; 1.1.35). Harpagon chooses his casket of treasure over his bride (Molière 93-94; 5.6.130). Volpone speaks of kissing "With adoration [. . .] every relic / Of sacred treasure in this blessed room" (Jonson 5; 1.1.11-13). Even the pathetic Silas Marner finds his coins occasion for "revelry": "He loved them all. He spread them out in heaps and bathed his hands in them; then he counted them and [. . .] felt their rounded outline between his thumb and fingers [. . .]" (Eliot 19; ch. 2). Only Grandet takes no joy in the mere presence of gold. Only he would pry the gold off an ornamented dressing case (Balzac 147) or part with all his gold, even at a profit. Grandet is the first prosaic miser, without a trace of aesthetic appreciation. The drabness of his obsession is epitomized in his remark "Life is a business" (152).

His obsession does have its appeal. To him, as to the other misers, money does bring happiness and vitality. Unlike them, though, he does not have to see his wealth to enjoy it. Indeed, his pleasure is not in gold at all but in scheming. His nature is venturesome and predatory, not retentive. His joy is in sharp dealing: in trading in stocks, in profiting from his brother's bankruptcy, in investing shrewdly, in besting rivals. Making money is a game, which he plays to the hilt and relishes thoroughly. No one in the novel has more zest than he.

Meortsnos 16

Works Cited

Balzac, Honoré de. <u>Eugénie Grandet</u>. Eugénie Grandet <u>and</u> The Curé of
    Tours. Trans. Merloyd Lawrence. Cambridge, MA: Riverside,
    1964. 1-180.

Eliot, George [Mary Ann Evans]. <u>Silas Marner</u>. Boston: Houghton,
    1962.

Jonson, Ben. <u>Volpone</u>. <u>Ben Jonson: Three Plays</u>. Ed. Brinsley
    Nicholson and C. H. Herford. New York: Mermaid-Hill, 1957.
    1-112.

Marlowe, Christopher. <u>The Jew of Malta</u>. <u>Christopher Marlowe: Five
    Plays</u>. Ed. Havelock Ellis. New York: Mermaid-Hill, 1956.
    198-266.

Molière [Jean Baptiste Poquelin]. <u>L'Avare</u>. Boston: Ginn, 1894.

9. Reference to Numbered Notes

Although numbered note reference is losing ground to parenthetical reference, many academic and general publications continue to use the numbered note system. This chapter gives a brief description of it.

This chapter presents only the basic rules for composing numbered notes and then gives various examples. The examples probably cover almost all the kinds of documents you will be acknowledging. Carefully match each of your notes with the appropriate example. For additional information on acknowledging a specific kind of work, see the corresponding entry in chapter 8, where more detailed information is given. Examples in this chapter match those in chapter 8: for instance, this chapter's *9.2.4* corresponds to *8.2.4* of chapter 8. To acknowledge a cited work beyond the scope of the presentation in these two chapters, see Joseph Gibaldi, *MLA Handbook for Writers of Research Papers*, 4th ed., New York: MLA, 1995, or Michael Meyer, *The Little, Brown Guide to Writing Research Papers*, 3d ed., Boston: Little, 1994.

9.1 General Description

Numbered notes are either endnotes (notes appearing at the end of the essay or chapter) or footnotes (notes appearing at the bottom of the page). If you are using the numbered note system, use endnotes rather than footnotes, unless you are required to use footnotes. Endnotes are almost as easy to consult as footnotes, and they are easier to type. Footnotes are still preferred for dissertations. Dissertations are often preserved on microfilm or microfiche, and it is far more convenient for the user of a microfilm projector to find notes at the bottom of a projected page than to stumble after them through a whir of slippery little rectangles. Although you will provide endnotes far more often than foot-notes, this chapter describes both.

- Endnotes are gathered at the end of the essay. Do not end your essay and begin your endnotes on the same sheet of paper. Instead, give endnotes a sheet or sheets of their own. Include these sheets in the pagination of your essay. Leave an extra line between the centered title "Notes" and the beginning of your list of notes. Double-space between all lines, within and between notes.

- Footnotes appear at the bottom of the page. Leave four lines between the text and the beginning of the first footnote. Single-space between the lines of a note and double-space be-tween notes.

- Notes are numbered consecutively throughout the essay.

- The beginning of each note is indented five spaces (like the start of a paragraph). Do not indent subsequent lines of the note. The format of a note reverses that of an entry in a list of works cited: the list-entry begins flush with the left margin of the text, with all later lines indented five spaces.

- The note-numeral is raised half a space above the line. Leave a single space between the numeral and the beginning of the note proper (in contrast to the corresponding numeral given in the body of the text: that numeral follows the citation without any intervening space). Do not put a period after the numeral.

- Each note begins with a capital letter and ends with a period.

The interior, too, of a note differs from that of a list-entry, as the following pair illustrates. First, a list-entry:

Carlyle, Thomas. <u>Sartor Resartus: The Life and
    Opinions of Herr Teufelsdröckh</u>. Ed. Charles
    Frederick Harrold. New York: Odyssey, 1937.

Next, a note:

> [1] Thomas Carlyle, <u>Sartor Resartus: The Life and Opinions of Herr Teufelsdröckh</u>, ed. Charles Frederick Harrold (New York: Odyssey, 1937) 298.

Notes differ from list-entries in the following ways:

- In a note there are four main divisions: author, title, publishing information, and textual reference. In a list-entry there are only three: author, title, and publishing information.

- In a note the names of the (first) author are given in the normal order. In a list-entry the first and last names of the (first) author are reversed.

- In a note the author's name is followed by a comma; in a list-entry the name is followed by a period. In a note the title of the work is followed by a parenthesis, which takes no punctuation after it, whereas in a list-entry the title is followed by a period.

- In a note publishing information on a book is framed in parentheses. In a list-entry publishing information is punctuated as if it were a sentence: the information begins with a capital letter and ends with a period.

- A note refers to a specific passage in the cited text. A list-entry refers to the whole book, the whole essay (with inclusive pages), or the whole set of volumes (including the number and inclusive dates of publication of the volumes in the set) in which the passage appears.

- Notes are arranged in the order in which the corresponding citations appear in the text. List-entries are arranged alphabetically according to authors' surname.

9.2 Examples

The style of your endnotes should be the same as the style of the notes given here, except that your notes should be double-spaced.

9.2.1   A book with one author:

¹ Eustace Chesser, <u>Salvation Through Sex: The Life and Work of Wilhelm Reich</u> (New York: Morrow, 1972) 213.

² Thomas J. Headlee, <u>The Mosquitoes of New Jersey and Their Control</u> (New Brunswick, NJ: Rutgers UP, 1945) 22-23.

9.2.2   A book with more than one author:

³ <u>Norton Anthology of Poetry</u>, ed Arthur M. Eastman, et al. (New York: Norton, 1970) 1196.

⁴ Arthur Raistrick and Bernard Jennings, <u>A History of Lead Mining in the Pennines</u> (London: Longman, 1965) 246-48.

9.2.3   An edition:

⁵ <u>Munching on Existence: Contemporary American Society through Literature</u>, ed. Robert Gliner and R. A. Raines (New York: Free, 1971) 14.

⁶ <u>An Anthology of Invective and Abuse</u>, ed. Hugh Kingsmill [Lunn] (New York: Dial, 1929) 221.

⁷ Ludwig Lavater, <u>Of Ghostes and Spirites Walking by Nyght</u>, ed. J. Dover Wilson and May Yardley (Oxford: Oxford UP, 1929) 77.

9.2.4   The standard edition of an author's works:

⁸ <u>The Poems of Arthur Hugh Clough</u>, ed. A. L. P. Norrington (London: Oxford UP, 1968) 242.

⁸ Arthur Hugh Clough, <u>The Poems</u>, ed. A. L. P. Norrington (London: Oxford UP, 1968) 242.

9.2.5   A second or later edition:

[9] Cleanth Brooks and Robert Penn Warren, Understanding Poetry, 4th ed. (New York: Holt, 1976) 200.

9.2.6   A book reprinted by a second publisher:

[10] George Orwell, 1984 (1949; rpt. New York: Signet-NAL, 1961) 202.

9.2.7   A translation:

[11] Karol Jalovec, Beautiful Italian Violins, trans. J. B. Kozác (London: Hamlyn, 1963) 24.

9.2.8   A work of more than one volume:

[12] E. Stuart Bates, Inside Out: An Introduction to Autobiography, 2 vols. (Oxford: Blackwell, 1937) 2: 143.

[13] Arthur Conan Doyle, "The Adventure of the Blanched Soldier," The Complete Sherlock Holmes, 2 vols. (Garden City, NJ: Doubleday, n.d.) 2: 1000-12.

[14] A Selection of African Prose, comp. W[ilfred] H[owell] Whitely (Oxford: Clarendon, 1964) 2: 69-84.

9.2.9   A play or long poem:

[15] Gammer Gurtons Nedle, Chief Pre-Shakespearean Dramas, ed. Joseph Quincy Adams (Cambridge, MA: Riverside, 1924) 478; 2.2.1-6.

Here the author is not cited because not known. When known, the author's name appears in the usual place, before the title of the work.

9.2.10 A shorter poem:

[16] Thomas Carew, "A Rapture," Norton Anthology of English Literature, ed. M. H. Abrams et al., 4th ed. (New York: Norton, 1979) 1: 1599.

[17] Wallace Stevens, "The River of Rivers in Connecticut," Collected Poems (New York: Knopf, 1957) 533.

9.2.11 An article in a periodical:

[18] A. F. Ruston, "A Note on Clorms," London Mathematical Society Journal 32 (1957): 110-12.

[19] R. D. Hill, "Pepper Growing in Johore," Journal of Tropical Geography 28.3 (1969): 37.

[20] Rudolph Dreikurs, "The Choice of a Mate," International Journal of Individual Psychology 1.4 (1935): 99-102.

[21] Vagn Flygers, "Hunters of White Whales," The Beaver Winter 1965: 35.

9.2.12 A daily or weekly newspaper or weekly or monthly magazine:

[22] "Mick Jagger Comments on Margaret Trudeau," Chicago Tribune, city ed., 15 Sept. 1977, sec. 1: 5.

[23] Gerald Lescelles, "The Chase of the Wild Fallow Deer," Nineteenth Century Oct. 1886: 509-10.

9.2.13 A review:

[24] Lola Romanucci-Ross, "The Old Lamplighters and the Case of the Curious Episteme: Fox and Freud and the Nature of Primatology," rev. of The

Red Lamp of Incest, by Robin Fox, Reviews in
Anthropology 8 (1981): 443.

[25] Leanne O. Wolff, rev. of Presidential Rhetoric: 1961-1980, ed. Theodore Windt, Presidential
Studies Quarterly 9 (1981): 589-90.

[26] "What to Feel Where," rev. of Abroad: A
Book of Travels, ed. Jon Evans, Times Literary
Supplement 16 Jan. 1969: 59.

9.2.14 A work in an anthology:

[27] Richard Wright, "Big Boy Leaves Home,"
An Introduction to Literature, ed. William Chace
and Peter Collier (San Diego: Harcourt, 1985)
155.

9.2.15 An electronically published book:

[28] John Ruskin, The King of the Golden River
(Champagne, IL: Project Gutenberg, 1996), 4
June 1998 <ftp//uiarchive.cso.uiuc.edu/pub/
etext/ gutenberg/etext96/tkogr10.txt>.

9.2.16 An article in an electronically published periodical:

[29] Ian Lancashire, "The Common Reader's
Shakespeare," Early Modern Literary Studies 3.3
Special Issue 2 (Jan. 1998): 4.11, 5 June 1998
<http://www.humanities.ualberta.ca/
emls/03-3/lancshak.html>.

9.2.17 A personal Web site:

[30] David A. Salomon, Hamlet in Hyperspace,
University of Connecticut, 3 March 1998, 5 June
1998 <http://www.sp.uconn.edu/~das93006/429/
home.html>.

9.2.18 A nonperiodical publication on CD-ROM:

[31] "Meerschaum," Oxford English Dictionary, 2nd ed., CD-ROM (Oxford: Oxford UP, 1992).

[32] Dickens, Charles, A Christmas Carol (London: Longman, 1991), CD-ROM (Foster City, CA: DynEd, 1994).

9.2.19 A work from a periodically published database on CD-ROM:

[33] Pamela Stephanie Loy, "Victoria's Camelot: Love, Work, and the Arthurian Revival," DAI 58 (1997): 3145A, U of Georgia, 1997, Dissertation Abstracts Ondisc, CD-ROM, UMI-Proquest, Dec. 1997.

9.2.15 Subsequent references:

Once a work has been treated fully in a first reference, do not repeat all the information every time you cite the work thereafter. If you cite only one work of an author, a subsequent note will consist of the author's surname and the new page number. Of course, if you cite more than one work by an author or if you cite more than one author with the same surname, your subsequent reference must be somewhat more informative, to avoid ambiguity.

[34] Jalovec 64.

[35] Stevens, "Tattoo" 81.

[36] Christina Rossetti 95.

A brief subsequent reference can often be given most economically in parentheses in your text. There, if there is no ambiguity as to what work you are citing, a parenthetical page number or line number is all you need give.

9.2.16 A short title:

> After an initial, complete citation of a work, you may re-
> fer to the work in your notes or in your text by a short ti-
> tle. For instance, after giving a complete note on
> William Hunt's <u>The Gaugers Magazine: Wherein the
> Foundation of His Art Is Briefly Explain'd and Illus-
> trated with Such Figures, as May Render the Whole In-
> telligible to a Mean Capacity</u>, you may refer thereafter to
> <u>Gaugers</u>. Similarly, <u>Dombey and Son</u> may be given as
> <u>Dombey</u>, and <u>The Ordeal of Richard Feverel</u> as <u>Ordeal</u>.

9.3   **Bibliography**

If you have acknowledged in your notes all the sources cited in
your text, then you need not include a bibliography, unless, of
course, your teacher requires one. In a paper with a bibliography
and numbered endnotes, the bibliography follows the notes. The
bibliography should begin a new page. It should contain all
works consulted, not just those mentioned in your notes. Label it
precisely: "List of Works Consulted," or "Annotated List of
Works Consulted." The form of the bibliography is the same as
that for a "List of Works Cited," described in chapter 8.

The following sample pages include several numbered notes.
Although they are given as footnotes, you will usually be providing endnotes. Footnotes are single-spaced; endnotes are
double-spaced. In every other respect endnotes take exactly the
same form as footnotes.

Meortsnos 2

Grandet is unique among the misers of
literature. Most are visionaries, with vivid
dreams of "infinite riches in a little room."[1]
Harpagon chooses his casket of treasure over
his bride.[2] Volpone speaks of kissing "With
adoration [. . .] every relic / Of sacred
treasure in this blessed room."[3] Even Silas
Marner finds his coins occasion for "revelry":
"He loved them all. He spread them out in
heaps and bathed his hands in them; then he
counted them and [. . .] felt their rounded
outline between his thumb and fingers
[. . .]."[4]

[1] The Jew of Malta, Christopher Marlowe:
Five Plays, ed. Havelock Ellis (New York:
Mermaid-Hill, 1956) 201; 1.1.35.

[2] Molière, L'Avare (Boston: Ginn, 1894)
93-94; 5.6.1-30.

[3] Volpone, Ben Jonson: Three Plays, ed.
Brinsley Nicholson and C. H. Herford (New
York: Mermaid-Hill, 1957) 5; 1.1.11-13.

[4] George Eliot, Silas Marner (Boston:
Houghton, 1962) 19.

Only Grandet feels no excitement in the mere
presence of gold. Only he would pry the gold
off a dressing case[5] or part with all his
gold, even at a profit. His joy is not in
gold at all but in sharp dealing. He is
venturesome and predatory, not retentive. He
has Volpone's love of scheming but without
Volpone's love of beautiful objects. Grandet
is the first prosaic miser, without a trace of
aesthetic delight. The drabness of his
obsession is epitomized in his remark "Life is
a business" (152).

[5] Honoré de Balzac, Eugénie Grandet,
Eugénie Grandet and The Curé of Tours, trans.
Merloyd Lawrence (Cambridge, MA: Riverside,
1964) 147.

10. Miscellaneous Points

Our language includes many incidental, arbitrary turns of phrase, which follow from no grand logical or grammatical scheme. We think *over* a proposition, but we do not think it *under*. We fall *in* love but not (what would seem better logic) *into* love, nor do we fall *in hate*. Such incidental peculiarities of a language are called *idioms*. This chapter presents in alphabetical order a list of especially troublesome idioms. It includes, too, a few other items that do not lend themselves to systematic treatment. Your dictionary, handbook, or teacher will help you with matters of usage not answered here.

10.1 Adjective, adverb.

A few verbs (e.g., *feel, smell, hear, speak, see*) can be followed by either an adjective or an adverb. The meaning of the sentence depends on which part of speech is chosen.

> I smell bad.

> I smell badly.

The adjective, "bad," proclaims that I am ripe for a shower; the adverb, "badly," that my sinuses are clogged. To distinguish, notice that the adjective is linked to the subject of the sentence ("bad I"), whereas the adverb is linked to the predicate verb ("smell badly").

10.2 Affect, effect.

Most frequently *affect* is a verb, meaning "influence" or "produce a change in," and *effect* is a noun, meaning "result": if you *affect* someone or something, you have an *effect* on him, her, or it. Much less often *effect* is used as a verb, *affect* as a noun. *Effect* as a verb means "produce" or "bring about": "The hurricane *effected* a change in his travel plans" (cf. "*affected* his travel plans"). As a noun, *affect* (with the accent on the first syllable) is a psychologists' term, meaning "perceivable indices of emotion": "The patient spoke without *affect* of his father's death." Except when among psychologists, say "feelings" or "emotions" instead. Here is a summary sentence: "Bête Middling's song so affected her audience that it had the effect of effecting a strong affect from them."

10.3   **A lot.**

A term appropriate to standard English but not to formal English (see 10.18, Diction). Write *a lot* as two words, not one.

10.4   **Ambiguous reference.**

A pronoun's reference to its antecedent should be unambiguous. The reader should not be left to choose among grammatically possible alternatives:

> Wuthering Heights is more enigmatic than Jane Eyre. I read *it* last summer.

Is "*Wuthering Heights*" the antecedent of "it," or is "*Jane Eyre*"? Had the passage read

> Wuthering Heights is more enigmatic than Jane Eyre, *which* I read last summer.

there would be no ambiguity, for "which" is placed where it can refer to "*Jane Eyre*" only. Now consider this passage:

> Patti hates Mitzi. *She* detests *her*, loathes *her*, abominates *her*.

The italicized pronouns may seem ambiguous: is the antecedent of "she" "Patti," or is it "Mitzi"? Here parallel syntax comes to the rescue, establishing "Patti" as the antecedent of "she," "Mitzi" of the three "her"'s. Parallelism is an acceptable way to resolve ambiguity. Finally we have

> Queen Victoria preferred Disraeli to Gladstone. She looked forward to *his* visits.

Does "his" refer to "Disraeli" or "Gladstone"? Attending to the sense of the passage, the reader decides that "Disraeli" is the likelier antecedent. But the problem should not be left for the reader to solve by means of nongrammatical considerations.

10.5 | Amount, number.

Amount refers to an undifferentiated mass; *number*, to countable things. We say, "The overturned tanker spilled a large *amount of Ovaltine* onto the highway," or "The overturned tanker spilled a large *number of gallons* of Ovaltine onto the highway." We say "an impossible *amount* of homework" or "an impossible *number* of homework assignments." The same principle governs the choice between *much* and *many*, *less* and *fewer*.

10.6 | As, like.

In formal English (see 10.18, Diction), whenever the choice between *as* and *like* arises, *like* is always a preposition, followed by an object. *As* is usually a conjunction, which may be followed by a clause.

> Act like me.

> Do as I do.

Do not use *like* to introduce a clause.

> **Wrong:**   . . . like a cigarette should.

In addition, *as*, like *like*, may be a preposition, with an object. Compare

> Jess Dandy went to the costume ball like a clown.

with

> Jess Dandy went to the costume ball as a clown.

The difference between the sentences is one of meaning, not grammatical construction. The former sentence remarks on how Jess was behaving; the latter mentions how he was dressed. The preposition *like* means "similar to" or "characteristic of"; the preposition *as* means "in the role or function of."

10.7 | **Basis.**

Basis is usually an empty filler: "Clayton washes his ears on a daily basis." Better: "Clayton washes his ears daily." One compact adverb does the work of a flaccid prepositional phrase. *Basis* is usually used baselessly (*not* "on a baseless basis").

10.8 | **Between, among.**

Between implies twoness; *among*, more than twoness. Do not keep this fact a secret between you and me. Let us broadcast it among our friends.

10.9 | **Cannot help but.**

A common but ungrammatical combination of two acceptable idioms. Use either

> I *cannot help thinking* that you and I inhabit different area codes.

or the rather stiff-sounding but trenchant

> I *cannot but think* that you are my Aunt Mildred.

10.10 | **Case.**

Pronouns (and, to a lesser extent, nouns) change spelling according to *case*: their role in the syntax of the sentence. There are three cases: *subjective* (or *nominative*), *possessive* (or *genitive*), and *objective*.

- A word is in the **subjective** case when it serves as subject of a sentence or clause, as subject complement, or as appositive to a word in the subjective case.

- A word is in the **possessive** case when spelled so as to show possession.

- A word is in the **objective** case when it serves as direct or indirect object, as object complement, as object of a preposition, or as appositive to a word in the objective case.

> The villain of the drama was *she*.

The pronoun is in the subjective case, because it serves as complement to the subject, "villain."

Bring back *my* bonny to *me*.

The first pronoun is in the possessive case. The second, as object of a preposition, is in the objective case.

10.11 | **Case of words in clauses.**

The case of a noun or pronoun in a clause is determined by its function in the clause, not by the function of the clause as a whole.

Give the busby to him.

Give the tangram to whoever asks for it.

In the first sentence the object of the preposition "to" is "him." "Him" is therefore in the objective case. In the second sentence the object of the preposition "to" is the whole clause "whoever asks for it." The clause is in the objective case. "Whoever" is the subject of the clause. As subject, it is in the subjective case.

10.12 | **Center around.**

A mixed idiom, which muddies metaphors. You either *revolve around* or *center on*.

10.13 | **Clichés.**

Clichés are stale, overused expressions, such as "the milk of human kindness," "Time will tell," and "red as a beet." Use only if you can breathe new life into them. Otherwise you will be barking up a dead horse.

10.14 | **Compare to, compare with.**

The first form implies similarity between apparently unlike things; the second form implies dissimilarity between apparently like things.

Let us compare the human race to a kudzu vine.

Let us compare Newt Gingrich with Robert Dole.

10.15   **Continual, continuous.**

The first means something like "very frequent"; the second means "without interruption." The chirping of a wren is continual; the hissing of a radiator, continuous.

10.16   **Contractions.**

Conventional contractions (e.g., *doesn't, haven't, you'll*) are perfectly appropriate in standard English, spoken and written. They are, however, usually out of place in formal English (see 10.18, Diction). Do not use contractions in standard academic writing.

10.17   **Dangling modifier.**

An ungrammatical construction, in which a modifier—usually an introductory elliptical clause or introductory verbal (infinitive, gerund, or participial) phrase—fails to modify the subject of the following clause. Here is a dangling participial phrase:

> Stooping to pick a roadside wildflower, a motorcycle almost laid me flat on my back.

The reader expects the subject of the main clause to reveal who is stooping. When the subject turns out to be "a motorcycle," the reader is first puzzled, then perhaps amused, at the writer's expense.

> Although tired, rest was not what Clarence needed now.

A dangling elliptical clause. *Rest* was not tired; *Clarence* was. Say so: "Although tired, *Clarence* did not need rest now."

> Steaming around the bend, the eager crowd could see President Truman's train approaching.

The crowd is not only eager but in full stride. A dangling participial phrase.

> To determine why sheep are flocculent, diet was the first factor we considered.   *[dangling infinitive phrase]*

> Instead of killing her, a different plan occurred to the wily fugitive.   *[dangling gerund phrase]*

Finally, a dangling modifier will occasionally follow the main clause.

> The four days were spent anxiously waiting the outcome of the trial.

10.18   Diction.

Choosing words suited to the occasion is a matter of *diction*. That a word is in the dictionary is not a license to use the word in any situation: a word appropriate to one set of conditions may not be appropriate to another. *Whereas* or *notwithstanding* would be out of place in the locker room; *oomph, persnickety,* or *itsy-bitsy,* in the *Papers of the Bibliographical Society of America.*

There are many kinds of English—many different modes of diction. Every geographical region, ethnic group, age group, occupation, and social class has its own mode of diction. And we change our English, more or less, as we move from one group to another.

Wise use of this booklet requires a distinction between two modes of diction: standard English and formal English. Standard English is the diction of most newspapers and magazines—the diction of general written discourse. Formal English, on the other hand, is the diction of academic, medical, legal, and business writing. Although the two modes of diction are the same in most respects, formal English is somewhat further removed from everyday speech than is standard English, perhaps more complex, and certainly more codified. Like all good writing, though, formal English should be concise and clear.

This booklet treats formal English, suitable for academic and professional writing. But formal English is not the only English worth knowing, nor is it suitable for every occasion.

10.19 | **Different from.**

Use the idiom *different from* rather than *different than*. *From* reinforces the idea of opposition inherent in *different* whereas *than* does not.

10.20 | **Disinterested.**

The innocent defendant craves a disinterested judge. *Disinterested* means "impartial," not "bored," and *disinterestedness* means "impartiality," not "boredom." *Uninterested*, not *disinterested*, is a synonym for *bored*. Do not use *disinterest*—ever.

10.21 | **Doublet without a distinction.**

Once said is enough said. Avoid writing like this:

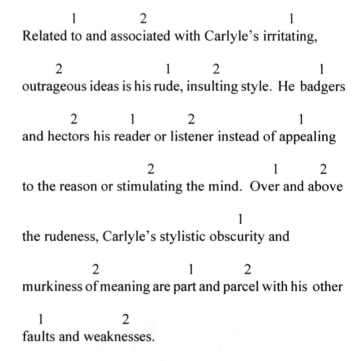

```
        1                2                           1
   Related to and associated with Carlyle's irritating,

        2             1       2                    1
   outrageous ideas is his rude, insulting style.  He badgers

        2         1       2                 1
   and hectors his reader or listener instead of appealing

                          2                   1       2
   to the reason or stimulating the mind.  Over and above

                                      1
   the rudeness, Carlyle's stylistic obscurity and

        2              1       2
   murkiness of meaning are part and parcel with his other

        1              2
   faults and weaknesses.
```

This writer never leaves home without both belt and suspenders.

10.22 | **Due to.**

Due is an adjective: "Sir, your bus is now due"; "This dime is your due reward"; "Have all due bills been paid?" In the next example "due" is a predicate adjective, modifying the subject, "failure," and the sentence is grammatically correct: "Henrietta's failure was due to poor eyesight."

There is, however, a movement afoot to use *due to* where *because of* would be proper: "Due to circumstances beyond our control, gasoline, when available, will be $473.98 a gallon." To the meekly ignorant, *due to* may sound more official or imposing than *because of.* It is, however, ungrammatical, for the adjective *due* modifies no noun. And it is pompous besides.

10.23 | **Each other, one another.**

The distinction between these terms is the same as that between *between* and *among* (see 10.8). *Each other* refers to two things; *one another*, to more than two. The danger lies in using *each other* where *one another* would be appropriate.

> Snow White and her wicked stepmother made *each other* miserable. The Seven Dwarfs, on the other hand, rejoiced in *one another's* company.

10.24 | **Enormity, enormousness.**

The first means "atrociousness"; the second means "hugeness." The danger is in using *enormity* where *enormousness* would be proper.

> **Wrong:**   The enormity of the mocha ice cream cone spoiled Lucille's appetite.

10.25 | **Fewer, less.**

Fewer refers to things that can be counted; *less*, to what cannot. Say "fewer hours," but "less time"; "fewer calories," but "less beer."

10.26 | **First-name reference.**

More and more people address and refer to more and more people by first name rather than by surname. The trend has not, however, seeped into literary discourse or other formal English. In your essay do not refer to George Gordon, Lord Byron as "George" or Jane Austen as "Jane." Instead, on first reference give the full name as it is commonly known ("Percy Bysshe

Shelley") and thereafter give just the surname ("Shelley"). Refer to fictional characters by the name that the author uses for them.

10.27 | **Fragment.**

A fragment is a group of words masquerading as a sentence (it begins with a capital letter and ends with a period, question mark, or exclamation point) but failing to satisfy one of the two criteria for a sentence. A sentence (a) contains a subject and predicate verb and (b) completes all the syntactic patterns it begins. The following fragments fail to meet the first criterion:

> Swallowed the lizard.   *[no subject]*

> The little girl with red pigtails.   *[no predicate verb]*

> Right before lunch.
> *[neither subject nor predicate verb]*

The following fragments contain a subject and predicate verb but fail to meet the second criterion:

> Knuckles resemble.
> *[transitive verb lacks direct object]*

> The koala scooted up the.
> *[preposition lacks object]*

> The trouble with Jacques Offenbach is that.
> *[noun clause introduced but absent]*

Often such fragments are dependent clauses that lack an independent clause:

> After the cows come home.

> When hell freezes over.

The subordinating conjunction ("after," "when") turns what would be a bona fide sentence ("The cows come home") into a fragment: in introducing a subordinate clause, the subordinating conjunction promises a main clause as well. Be careful, though, to distinguish between subordinating conjunctions and conjunctive adverbs: the latter do not subordinate their clause so do not promise an additional clause:

> Although [*s.c.*] Brian was shy.   *[fragment]*
>
> However [*c.a.*], Brian was shy.   *[sentence]*
>
> Because [*s.c.*] George is gorgeous.   *[fragment]*
>
> Therefore [*c.a.*] George is gorgeous.   *[sentence]*

Because a subordinating conjunction must open its clause whereas a conjunctive adverb need not, you can discriminate between these connectives by seeing whether the word makes sense when appearing elsewhere in its clause. "George is because gorgeous" is garbled English, whereas "George is, therefore, gorgeous" is an acceptable word order.

Finally, although almost all fragments are considered faults, terse fragments, like "By all means," "Not on your life," and "Quite the contrary," are acceptable, even in formal English. If, though, your reader wonders whether your fragment is a rhetorical grace or a grammatical lapse, you have used a fragment improperly.

10.28 | Gerund, possessive before.

The gerund is a verb ending in *ing* and used as a noun. When it is preceded by a noun or pronoun pertaining to it, the noun or pronoun takes the possessive case.

> Melvin was distracted by *your* whimpering.
>
> *Chester's* planting corn brought joy to the hearts of the neighborhood raccoons.

But distinguish between the following two sentences:

> The *man eating* the meatloaf solved the mystery of the missing engagement ring.
>
> The *man's eating* the meatloaf solved the mystery of the missing engagement ring.

"Man" is the subject of the first sentence, and "eating" is a present participle—not a gerund—modifying man. The gerund "eating" is the subject of the second. Both sentences are grammatically correct. The choice between such sentences depends on exactly what one means to say.

10.29   **Gobbledegook.**

Gobbledegook means "turkey droppings." Applied to speaking or writing, it means "inflated, pretentious prose." Gobbledegook is using the long word or syntactic construction instead of the short one in an effort to impress others with one's importance. Gobbledegook is saying

> It is only to be expected that one regularly and habitually refraining from reinstituting the removable closure device discoverable, when said device is purchased, at the anterior extremity of a dentifrice module is liable to be the receptor of frequent episodes of hostile affect generated by proximal associates.

instead of

> Repeatedly neglecting to recap the toothpaste makes one's house mates angry.

Do not confuse gobbledegook with formal English, which should be at least as clear and concise as any other mode of diction.

10.30   **Hanged, hung.**

Pictures (and other inanimate things) are *hung*; some unfortunate people (and other creatures) are *hanged*.

10.31   **Homo sapiens.**

Reserve *human* and *individual* for use as adjectives, not nouns. Nouns that refer to our species include *human being(s), humanity, humankind, person(s)* and *people*. Because *person* is a stolen, makeshift singular for *people*, and *persons* is sometimes awkward as the plural of *person*, avoid, if you can, a shift in number with either noun. *Man* and *mankind* are now in disfavor for implying that one gender can subsume the other.

10.32 | **Hopefully.**

Do not use *hopefully* to mean "I hope."

> **Wrong:**   Hopefully the princess kissed the toad.

The sentence is ambiguous: "hopefully" can mean either "I hope" ("I hope the princess kissed the toad") or "in a hopeful mood" ("Expectantly the princess kissed the toad").

The ambiguity comes about because an adverb can modify either the rest of its sentence (or clause) or a term within the sentence (or clause). The meaning of most adverbs prevents ambiguity:

> Unfortunately, newt juice is hard to find.

"Unfortunately," which modifies the rest of its sentence, makes no sense if we try to make the word modify any other term. But *hopefully*, as well as *importantly, surely, obviously,* and some other adverbs, is liable to ambiguity:

> Importantly, Major Catastrophe abandoned his post during the battle.

> Surely Donald drove Mickey to Disneyland.

Did the major leave with pomp and circumstance, or was his leaving crucial to the outcome of the battle? Did Donald drive to Disneyland expertly, or is the fact that he drove there a certainty? To avoid such ambiguity, be circumspect in using adverbs to modify whole sentences or clauses.

10.33 | **How, That.**

In introducing a clause, avoid using *how* where *that* is appropriate. *How* refers to manner, whereas *that* (when it serves as subordinating conjunctive) merely announces the advent of a fact.

> Lucinda, do you remember *how* we used to climb the old sycamore when we were childhood friends?

If the speaker is referring to the technique that she and Lucinda used to climb the tree, the sentence is accurate. But if the speaker is merely asking her old friend to recall occasions when the two climbed the tree, she would have spoken more clearly had she phrased her question thus:

> Lucinda, do you remember *that* we used to climb the old sycamore when we were childhood friends?

10.34 | **Imply, infer.**

Imply means "to suggest without stating directly"; *infer* means "to conclude on the basis of gathered evidence." The reader infers what the book implies.

10.35 | **Incomparable words.**

The meaning of some adjectives and adverbs prevents their having a comparative or superlative degree. For instance, something either is or is not perfect; to say that Divinia is "more perfect" than Angela does not make strict sense. Other such words of fixed degree are *unique(ly), basic(ally), round, square(ly), accurate(ly), correct(ly), final(ly), full(y), empty (emptily)*, and *dead*. To show differences with respect to these qualities, resort to terms of approximation: "more nearly full," not "fuller"; "the most nearly dead," not "deadest."

> **Wrong:**   *The Style Booklet* is rather unique.
>
> **Right:**   *The Style Booklet* is very strange.

10.36 | **It is . . . that.**

Because the *it is . . . that* construction is wordy, avoid it unless it is needed for emphasis. Do not let the construction become a stylistic mannerism. Compare the bland

> It is the mighty Casey who has struck out.

with the plangent, heart-rending

> Mighty Casey has struck out.

10.37 | **Its, it's.**

Its, without an apostrophe, is a possessive pronoun. If tempted to confer an apostrophe upon it, remember its siblings, *his* and *hers*, which also take no apostrophe. *It's*, with an apostrophe, is the contraction for "it is."

It's a shame that the kitten has lost *its* mittens.

If you are writing in formal English, use *it is*, not *it's* (see 10.16, Contractions, and 10.18, Diction).

10.38 | **Lay, lie.**

Let us lay this little problem to rest once and for all. To *lie* is the infinitive form of two verbs. They have different meanings and different principal parts. One verb means "to tell an untruth."

Present tense:	*lie*	People lie about their age.
Past tense:	*lied*	The Greeks lied to the Trojans.
Past participle:	*lied*	Altruists have always lied more than egotists.

The other verb—the one that causes the trouble—means "to recline."

Present tense:	*lie*	I lie on the bank of the Fenton River.
Past tense:	*lay*	In April I lay on the golden sand at Hammonasset Beach.
Past participle:	*lain*	I have always lain about whenever I have had the chance.

To lay means "to set (something) down." It is transitive, whereas *to lie* in either of its senses is intransitive.

Present tense:	*lay*	May I lay my pen on the clean blotter?
Past tense:	*laid*	Yesterday I mislaid my wallet.
Past participle:	*laid*	Winston had laid his Stetson on the hood of the Datsun.

Two matters cause the latter two verbs to be confused: (a) The past tense of *to lie* and the present tense of *to lay* are both *lay*. And (b) the reflexive form of *to lay* can mean "to recline": "I have always laid myself down"; "Now I lay me down to sleep."

The two verbs *to sit* (*sat, sat*) and *to set* (*set, set*) are similar in meaning and relationship to *lie* (*lay, lain*) and to *lay* (*laid, laid*), respectively, but they are less troublesome. You may find *sit* and *set* helpful parallels as you grapple with *lie* and *lay*.

10.39 Metaphors, mixed.

All writers mix metaphors constantly; they cannot help doing so. Nevertheless, try to make your images harmonize and, where harmony is impracticable, try to make transitions inconspicuous. Avoid passages in which images war with one another, as in "The new mayor will stamp out the hemorrhage in the can of worms hanging like a sword over city hall."

10.40 Misplaced modifier.

In speech inaccurate placement of modifiers can sometimes be rectified through intonation; in writing, though, no voice comes to the rescue. If we write

Marjorie only expects Janet's sincere thanks.

the reader, deprived of intonation, tries to make "only" modify "expects": Marjorie expects the thanks but does not deserve them? But will not receive them? Or is it "Marjorie only" who expects thanks? The writer should place "only" where it modifies "thanks" only:

Marjorie expects Janet's sincere thanks only.

The power of placement can be illustrated by playing with *only* and the three little words "I love you":

> *Only* I love you.

Translation: I love you, but no one else does.

> I *only* love you.

Translation: either the preceding sentiment, or this one: I love you but do not like or respect you.

> I love *only* you.

Translation: I love you and you alone—stress on "you."

> I love you *only*.

Translation: I love you and you alone—stress on "alone."

We see that a modifier can appear too early. It can also appear too late, modifying an inappropriate, intervening term:

> I was hit by a little fellow in a small car with a big mouth.

"With a big mouth" attaches itself to the nearest preceding noun, "car," rather than to "fellow," which the writer meant to modify. One corrected version: "A little fellow with a big mouth hit me with his small car." Prepositional phrases in series are especially liable to ambiguous placement, but clauses and other phrases can also be misplaced:

> Rupert's smile flashed in the light of the Transylvanian moon, *gleaming with long, silver teeth.*

The teeth belong with Rupert's smile but latch on instead to the moon. One corrected version: "Gleaming with long, silver teeth, Rupert's smile flashed in the light of the Transylvanian moon."

When a modifier is placed where it can modify more than one term, it is said to be "squinting." We have already seen that "I only love you" can be taken two ways. Here are other examples:

Tell her *when she stops crying* I am sorry.

The questions that you ponder *deeply* concern all humanity.

Bruno offered *on his own* to go to the taxidermist's.

Relocating the squinting modifiers resolves the ambiguities.

Also see 10.17, Dangling modifier, and 10.56, Split infinitive, special types of misplaced modifier.

10.41   **Parallelism.**

Similarity of ideas should be reflected in similarity of syntax and, where it helps to do so, repetition of terms. Consider this passage:

> People drive more slowly than they used to. OPEC's manipulating our oil supply has led us to drive smaller cars. Americans now travel less, too.

The thoughts are scattered. The sentences cry out for parallelism:

Because OPEC has manipulated the oil supply,
Americans drive   smaller cars
                         at slower speeds
                         over shorter distances   than before.

The result is not only clearer but more informative. The reader is given the same facts as before, plus their relationship. Parallelism is the tacit communication of order.

So when parallel structure is appropriate—when ideas are like or opposed—balance a word or term with a word or term of the same syntactic type: balance a noun with a noun, a prepositional phrase with a prepositional phrase, an adverbial clause with an adverbial clause, and so forth.

Not parallel: Lacrosse is a sport   with nonstop action
                          but   that draws few spectators.

"But that," together with its clause, implies a preceding, parallel "that" clause. The sentence could be mended in a number of ways. It could take parallel objects of the preposition "with":

Lacrosse is a sport   with   nonstop action
                      but   few spectators.

It could take parallel adjective clauses:

Lacrosse is a sport   that produces nonstop action
                  but   that draws few spectators.

The sentence could take a parallel compound predicate:

Lacrosse   produces nonstop action
     but   draws few spectators.

Often parallelism is a grammatical necessity. The elements of a series (including lists) should be syntactically parallel. And the elements of correlative constructions (e.g., *both . . . and, either . . . or, neither . . . nor, not only . . . but also*) should be syntactically parallel:

Not parallel: Twylla is   not only   the brightest star in
                                          the Hollywood
                                          firmament
                          but also   politically active.

"Not only" leads to "star," a predicate noun; "but also," to "active," a predicate adjective. Furthermore, "brightest" in the first term promises another adjective in the superlative degree in the second term. Better:

Parallel: Twylla is   not only   the brightest star in
                                          the Hollywood
                                          firmament
                          but also   the busiest
                                          campaigner
                                          for animal rights.

Parallelism keeps the reader on the writer's line of thought.

10.42 | **Positive(ly), negative(ly).**

Paired, *positive* and *negative* are mathematical terms, indicating direct opposition. They are most useful when applied to situations reducible to simple duality. When speaking of matters too various and complex to be reduced to a twofold scheme, avoid statements such as "I feel negative toward her" or "He thinks very positively about the plan." More specific alternatives are easy to find: "I loathe her"; "I disagree with her opinion"; "I disapprove of her flirting"; "She is not qualified for the job"; "I am jealous of her naturally curly hair." Avoid, too, using *positively* as a mere intensifier, as in "Wilma was positively exhausted." The root meaning of *positive* is "settled" or "established," and the word works well when the root meaning is implied: "I have positive [unshakable] proof that you are Phil Wanted, the desperado"; "He was positive [set in his belief] that the tooth fairy would reward him." In voting, the opposite of "negative" is "affirmative."

10.43 | **Possessive, double.**

Pondering the double possessive has provided grammarians untold hours of wholesome diversion. Expressions such as "the pralines of Harold's," "twelve handkerchiefs of hers," and "this old friend of mine" seem redundant. The preposition, *of*, already indicates possession, so why add the *'s*, which also indicates possession? Why is the object of the preposition given in the possessive form and not the objective?

The double possessive is firmly rooted in English and allows for distinctions such as that between "the portrait of my uncle" and "the portrait of my uncle's": the first phrase marks "uncle" as the subject of the portrait, and the second phrase, as the owner. "What do you want of me?" means something quite different from "What do you want of mine?"

To test a double possessive for appropriateness, see whether one can substitute *among* for *of*: "the pralines *among* Harold's [pralines]," "twelve handkerchiefs *among* hers [her handkerchiefs]," "the portrait *among* my uncle's [portraits]." The test shows that the term modified by the double-possessive prepositional phrase—"pralines," "handkerchiefs," "portrait,"—is considered as a member of a class. And the possessive object of the preposition *of*—"Harold's," "hers," "uncle's,"— modifies the name of the implicit class itself, which is inferred from the name of the member: the class *pralines* is inferred from its named member, "pralines"; the class *friends,* from its named member, "friend," and so forth. The member of a class can make up the whole class, and the class can consist of only one member: "Frieda is the only daughter of my teacher's." The sentence still considers "daughter" as a member of the class *daughters*.

The grammarian Otto Jespersen has noted that when a double possessive is appropriately used, one can substitute *who is* (or the appropriate similar term, such as *who are, that is, which are*) for the preposition *of.* The examples given above become "the pralines *that are* Harold's," "twelve handkerchiefs *that are* hers," "this old friend, *who is* mine," "the portrait, *which is* my uncle's."

Combining the tests gives in full-figure phrasing the meaning of the double possessive: "the pralines *among* the pralines *that are* Harold's pralines"; "the only daughter *among* the daughters *who are* my teacher's daughters." Only in constructions that could be rendered thus is the double possessive appropriate.

A helpful test example is Edgar Allan Poe's title "The Fall of the House of Usher." We would say, "the collapse of the barn of Ed Soja's," so why does not Poe write, "the fall of the house of Roderick Usher's"? He does not because he means something different. He does not mean, "the fall of the house among the houses that are Roderick Usher's houses." He means instead, "the fall of the house *named* 'Usher.'" Poe's *house* denotes "family line," as in the expressions "House of York" and "House of Windsor." This meaning resists our tests for the double possessive. Although Poe's story describes in detail the decay and collapse of the structure itself, the structure symbolizes the Usher family line, the fall of which is Poe's true subject.

10.44 | **Reason . . . because.**

Reason, because, and *why* imply one another. Two or all three of the words in the same construction are redundant:

> **Wrong:** The reason he ate the toad was because it was there.
>
> **Even worse:** The reason why he ate the toad was because it was there.
>
> **Right:** The reason he ate the toad was that it was there.
>
> **Even better:** He ate the toad because it was delicious.

10.45 | **Redundancy.**

Fear that the reader will not notice what one has just said produces a kind of wordiness called *redundancy.* Concise writing avoids redundancy. Specific kinds of redundancy are treated in 10.21 (Doublet without a distinction) and 10.44 (Reason . . . because). The following list of examples, all culled from students' essays, should help you recognize and avoid redundancy: "clearly evident"; "fluctuates back and forth"; "her inner thoughts"; "she stands alone with nobody"; "the possessions that they have"; "significant meaning"; "recalled memories of what once was"; "remembering these memories"; "dismounts his horse"; "beckoned her with a wave"; "self-educated myself"; "the written language in which he writes"; "larger in size"; "plans ahead"; "lags behind"; "sufficiently adequate"; "sufficient enough"; "seriously grave"; "on the outer surface"; "to match two people together as a couple"; "to move forward and advance towards progression."

10.46 | **Referentless pronouns.**

Be sure all your pronouns refer to specific nouns.

> The beach was crowded. Mosquitoes were everywhere. And there was sand in all the sandwiches. *This* spoiled the outing.

That "this" is a careless, over-the-shoulder wave, referring to no specific word but rather to "all that back there." Such a practice works passably for casual chatter, but it does discourage sharply focused thinking. Formal prose and a rigorous argument would require something like "These annoyances spoiled the outing." Other pronouns in especial danger of going referentless are *that, which,* and *it.*

10.47 | **Seems, appears, apparently.**

Inappropriate use of *seems, appears,* and *apparently* betrays timidity and causes confusion. Unless a distinction between appearance and reality is called for, do not use *seems, appears,* or *apparently.*

> Although at first Emma Woodhouse appears self-centered, seemingly treating friends as mere playthings, she does finally seem to grow genuinely interested, almost, in the apparent welfare of others, perhaps.

The sentence suggests that Emma was not really self-centered, did not really treat her friends carelessly, and did not really become interested in them. Better:

> Although at first Emma is self-centered, treating friends as mere playthings, she does finally grow genuinely interested in their welfare.

10.48 | **Sesquipedalian words.**

Sesquipedalian illustrates its own meaning: "a foot and a half long." A sesquipedalian word is one longer than necessary. When is a word too long? When there is a quite satisfactory shorter or less pretentious alternative. Almost always *utilize* is a sesquipedalian word, because *use* says all that is needed. Similarly, almost always *eventuate* should yield to *happen; reside,* to *live; parameters,* to *limits* or *conditions; purchase,* to *buy; virtually,* to *almost; impact* as a verb, to *affect; precipitation,* to *rain.*

At issue is not really length but clarity. Readers grasp plain words more easily than they do ornate ones. Writers who favor sesquipedalian words tend to be more concerned with impressing their readers than with informing them. See also 10.29, Gobbledegook.

10.49 | **Sex talk.**

Gone are the days when the masculine form of the personal pronoun in the third person singular (*he, his, him*) could stand for all human beings, including female ones.

> Every lawyer in the Greater Willimantic Area will raise *his* voice against this unfair legislation.

Although everyone knows that there are female lawyers in the Greater Willimantic Area, the stereotypical lawyer is male, and using *his* reinforces the stereotype. Not wishing to distract or offend readers or perpetuate stereotypes, the modern writer avoids this use of the pronoun. Unfortunately, there is no generally accepted third-person singular pronoun that denotes both genders—would that there were. When, however, you find yourself in a situation that requires one, there are ways, some better than others, to solve the problem. A passable solution satisfies those who expect the language to give women equal billing with men and those who expect to read good English, including consistency in syntax. An even better solution also keeps readers undistracted from your line of thought, because unaware that the problem has ever arisen. Here is one attempt at a solution:

> Every lawyer in the Greater Willimantic Area will raise *their* voice against this unfair legislation.

Their succeeds in including both genders but wreaks havoc on syntax: the plural *their* disagrees in number with the singular *lawyer*, its antecedent (see 10.52, Shifts in number). The disagreement muddies the prose, impedes all readers, and dismays literate ones. The recasting of the sentence trades one peeved readership for another. Here is another revision:

> Every lawyer in the Greater Willimantic Area will raise *his/her* voice against this unfair legislation.

Many writers, readers, and teachers find *his/her* (along with *s/he*) an appropriate solution to the problem. Others, though, find it an excrescence on the language (see 4.13, The Slash). A major weakness of *his/her* is that it calls attention to itself as a solution to the original problem. When readers encounter *his/her*, their attention is diverted from the content of the writer's prose to the issues that led to the creation of the construction. Let us try again:

> Every lawyer in the Greater Willimantic Area will raise *his or her* voice against this unfair legislation.

The construction includes both genders and is somewhat less conspicuous than *his/her*. But it is cumbersome. The occasional *his or her* may see the writer through, but frequent use of the phrase makes prose ponderous. We press onward:

> *All lawyers* in the Greater Willimantic Area will raise *their* voices against this unfair legislation.

At last! Recasting the sentence so that the antecedent is plural solves the problem, and it does so inconspicuously. No one is offended; no one is distracted. Not all such *he, his, him* problems can be solved by resorting to the plural, but very many can. For those that cannot, the resourceful writer can rephrase in some other way:

> Every lawyer in the Greater Willimantic Area will *object vociferously* to this unfair legislation.

Finally, in many sentences the problem can be avoided by discovering that the sentence works perfectly well without the offensive pronoun or any substitute for it:

Problem sentence:	Each student turned in *his* [*their? his/her? his or her?*] homework.
Simple solution:	Each student turned in *the* homework.

In sum, the three best ways to treat the problem are (1) switching to the plural, (2) rephrasing otherwise, and (3) discovering that there need not be a problem after all.

10.50 | **Shall, will.**

Many writers use these words in such a way as to achieve a distinction not deftly obtainable in other ways. When merely referring to the future, they write

I shall . . .   we shall . . .
you will . . .   you will . . .
he (she, it) will . . .   they will . . .

On Monday we <u>shall</u> go to the dogs.

Some day Lassie <u>will</u> come home again.

But when expressing determination, they write

I will . . .   we will . . .
you shall . . .   you shall . . .
he (she, it) shall . . .   they shall . . .

My good man, you <u>shall</u> serve us *coquilles St. Jacques à la parisienne*, else I <u>will</u> never enter Hardee's again.

She <u>shall</u> be mine, and I <u>will</u> make
A Lady of my own.
                              (William Wordsworth)

I <u>will</u> not cease from Mental Fight,
Nor <u>shall</u> my Sword sleep in my hand
Till we have built Jerusalem
In England's green & pleasant land
                              (William Blake)

10.51 | **Shifts in mood.**

The grammatical term *mood* has nothing to do with the emotions: it means merely "mode": the mode of a predicate verb. The *mood* of a verb is its change in form—in spelling—to indicate whether its clause makes a statement (*indicative* mood), gives an order (*imperative* mood), or hypothesizes a case known to be untrue or merely supposed to be true (*subjunctive* mood).

Be consistent. Once you establish a mood, maintain it, unless what you are saying requires a change. Avoid shifts like these:

> If Donald *were* not pouting and Marla *was* not
> in a rage. . . .
>> *[improper shift from subjunctive to indicative]*

> *Wash* your socks, and *you should also wash* your ears.
>> *[improper shift from imperative to indicative]*

But the shift in the next example is justified by the shift in meaning:

> Wash your ears: there are potatoes growing in them.
>> *[proper shift from imperative to indicative]*

10.52 **Shifts in number.**

Problematical shifts in number involve pronouns and verbs.

10.52.1. Pronouns.

A pronoun should agree in number with its antecedent.

> **Wrong**: *Everybody* should bring *their* bathing
>   suit.

The antecedent of the pronoun "their" is "everybody," which is singular. So "their" should also take a singular form: "his," or "her."

> **Wrong**: *Each* of the Roman soldiers showed
>   *their* rank by the height of *their* shoes.

The antecedent of the two "their"'s is "each," not "soldiers." "Each" is singular, so the two pronouns should also be singular: "his."

> **Right**: *Each* of the Roman soldiers showed *his*
>   rank by the height of *his* shoes.

10.52.2 Verbs.

A verb should agree in number with its subject.

> **Wrong:** Often a *group* of words *come* between
> the subject and the predicate verb.

The subject of the sentence is "group," not "words." "Group" is singular, so the predicate verb, "come," should be singular also:

> **Right:** Often a *group* of words *comes* between
> the subject and the predicate verb.

Even if a singular subject is followed by a prepositional phrase introduced by *with, along with, besides, in addition to*, or *as well as*, the subject remains singular, as does the verb. In the following example, the singular predicate verb (italicized) agrees with the singular subject (also italicized). The intervening prepositional phrase, although long, does not affect the number of the verb:

> *Meryl Streep*, in addition to Magic Johnson, Kofi Annan, Brad Pitt, Nykesha Sales, John Roland, Michael Milken, Charo, Secretariat, Luciano Pavarotti, Ellen Goodman, Bugs Bunny, and Hélène Cixous, sometimes *eats* vegetables.

10.53 Shifts in person.

Be consistent. Once you establish a grammatical person—first, second, or third—maintain it unless your meaning justifies a change.

> **Wrong:** First *one* goes two miles on Codfish
> Falls Road. Then *you* turn left onto
> Bone Mill Road. After the big green
> barn *he* bears right onto Dog Lane.

No complicated concept is involved here: the writer has merely forgotten what he has said.

10.54 | **Shifts in tense.**

Be consistent. Once you establish a tense, maintain it unless your meaning justifies a change.

> **Wrong:**   Albee *wrote*. . . . In the next scene he
>   *writes*. . . .

Writers on literature or history are especially prone to shift between the present tense and the past tense. They do so because they are not comfortable with the convention of using the present tense to talk about past events, fictional or actual. But it is wholly proper and convenient to do so. Even at this late date Chaucer still "writes," King Lear "rages," and Hannibal still "crosses" the Alps.

Shifts in tense are, of course, quite appropriate when the meaning requires them:

> **Right:**   For supper Zane *ate* three large pizzas.
>   Tomorrow he *will be* sorry.

10.55 | **Since, while.**

To express logical connections, thinkers have always resorted to terms that apply to space and time: "It *follows* that this is the best of all possible worlds." As a result, some such terms have taken on a double meaning:

> *Since* it is raining, Wanda's car will not start.

"*Because* it is raining," or "*After* it started to rain?" Is the connection causal or merely temporal? Whenever *since* is ambiguous (as in the example), use another conjunction instead.

Although *while*, too, can be ambiguous, it is seldom so when making a temporal connection. Reserve *while* for temporal connections and use an unambiguous synonym (e.g., *although, whereas*) for other, more abstract connections:

While Rome fiddled, Nero burned.
> *["While" refers to time.]*

Although Rome fiddled, Nero burned.
> *["Although" marks an opposition.]*

10.56 **Split infinitive.**

An infinitive is a verbal introduced by *to: to twist, to harmonize, to be vermiculated.* An infinitive is "split" when a modifier stands between *to* and the infinitive: *to opportunely fertilize, to discreetly sweat.* Besides respectable precedent, common sense argues for splitting infinitives: a modifier so placed is never ambiguous as to referent, whereas in any other position a modifier of an infinitive is in danger of being ambiguous in reference or of causing awkward phrasing.

Nevertheless, if there is an alternative wording that is neither ambiguous nor awkward, do not split an infinitive. The convention not to do so is still strong. Because a split infinitive annoys some readers and distracts many more, say "mercilessly to keelhaul" or "to keelhaul mercilessly," not "to mercilessly keelhaul."

10.57 **Terms of, in.**

Reserve *in terms* of for references to actual, specifiable terms. If there are no such terms, *in terms of* is just an empty filler. Your prose is more concise without it.

Flabby:	The Baron admires Belinda in terms of her artificially curly hair.
Firm:	The Baron admires Belinda for her artificially curly hair.
Flabby:	The Baron distresses Belinda in terms of furtively snipping off one of her curls with a pair of scissors.
Firm:	The Baron distresses Belinda by furtively snipping off one of her curls with a pair of scissors.

10.58 | **That, which.**

When presented with the choice between the relative pronouns *that* and *which* for introducing an adjective clause, you increase the clarity of your prose by using *that* to introduce restrictive clauses, *which* to introduce nonrestrictive clauses. The choice between them reinforces a distinction already marked by the presence or absence of commas. See 3.2.

> Everyone signed the petition, *which* demanded reduced taxes, more services, and no governmental intervention.

> The play *that* you saw on Broadway is not the one *that* eventually opened in Storrs.

Because writers tend to overuse *which*, in practice the distinction involves what has come to be called "*which*-hunting": seeking out inappropriate *which*'s in one's prose and putting *that*'s in their place. Occasionally, however, *which* is used even in restrictive clauses:

• In a *that which* construction:

> The snowmobile you need is *that which* will give you the most miles per dollar.

• In a *for which, of which,* or other introductory prepositional construction (*that* as a relative pronoun is fiercely proud of place: if it cannot be the first word in a clause, it will not appear at all):

> The question *on which* he wrote his dissertation was why most pencils are six-sided rather than cylindrical.

A final note: *which* never refers to people. *That* may refer to people, but *who* (*whom*), used restrictively or nonrestrictively, is usually the best relative pronoun to use in reference to people:

> **Esteemed:**   the girl *whom* I marry
>
> **Tolerated:**   the girl *that* I marry
>
> **Disdained:**   the girl *which* I marry

10.59 | **There is (are).**

There are too many sentences that begin, "There are. . . ." To see why, compare the previous sentence with "Too many sentences begin, 'There are. . . .'" "There are" is wordy and usually unnecessary. Merely announcing the existence of something that follows, the construction postpones and obscures the information that matters. See also 10.36, It is . . . that.

10.60 | **To, too, two**

To is a preposition ("*to* the barricades") or the sign of an infinitive ("*to* palpitate"). **Too** is an adverb. It means "also" ("I, *too*, saw the alien spacecraft") or "overly" ("Alfred is *too* worried about his sweaty palms"). **Two** is a number ("I have a table for *two*").

> The *two* girls, *too*, were *too* clever *to* go *to* school in their tutus.

10.61 | **Train of thought.**

No paper should be without one. A good essay is a mental journey, with a starting point, a clearly marked route, and at journey's end a satisfying view. The first drafts of even the best essays are seldom easy or direct journeys. Usually they are pioneering explorations, involving wrong turns, blind alleys, will-o'-the-wisps, and much meandering. After writing such a draft, determine first exactly where your explorations have led you. Then retrace your steps, straightening the path, eliminating all wrong turns, and marking the route so that readers can follow it easily. If you can direct readers to your culminating insight without making them repeat the pain and confusion of your first explorations, they will indeed bless you.

10.62 | **Umbilical cord, cutting the.**

An essay should be free-standing. It should make sense to a reader unfamiliar with the assignment sheet that provoked it or with class discussion on the topic. Therefore do not, for example, begin your essay in this fashion: "One answer to the question might be. . . ." Do not declare, "The poem illustrates everything you said in class about odes." If an idea given on the assignment sheet or in class is important to your paper, write it out; do not merely allude to it.

10.63 | **Voice.**

Do not be put off by the word *voice* here: it means merely "mode." When a transitive verb is in a form that requires it to take a direct object, it is said to be **active**, or in the *active voice*. A sentence or clause with an active verb can be reorganized, with the (sometimes only implicit) direct object becoming the subject of the verb. The former subject becomes an object of a preposition or disappears. In addition, the verb changes its form. The verb of a sentence or clause thus reorganized is said to be **passive**, or in the *passive voice*.

> **Active:** The lonesome yodeler roams the loamy dunes.
>
> **Passive:** The loamy dunes are roamed by the lonesome yodeler.
>
> **Active:** The Fairfield Fieldmice had lost again.
>
> **Passive:** Another game had been lost by the Fairfield Fieldmice.

Use the active voice whenever you can. A sentence with an active verb is always shorter and seems more direct than its counterpart in the passive. True, the passive is sometimes the better choice. It is so when it emphasizes what is important when the active cannot do so. But all too often writers use the passive in an attempt to sound official, intelligent, or otherwise important:

> It is to be hoped that henceforth such conduct will not be engaged in again.

The sentence uses two passive constructions. Compare it with the following sentence, which uses two active ones:

> I hope you quit stealing hubcaps.

The second sentence, which even gives more information than the first, contains six words; the first, fifteen. Hence at least sixty percent of the first sentence consists of inert natural gases. They cause the first sentence to pass over our heads, while the second strikes home.

Using the passive voice to avoid saying "I" is a widespread stylistic practice. Much scientific writing justifiably avoids using "I," because such writing details experiments that involve many operations. Introducing all the operations with "I" would deflect attention from the experiment to the experimenter, who would sound conceited.

In other situations, though, the passive enables speakers to evade personal responsibility for their words or deeds. Using the passive voice for this purpose is an act of skulking cowardice. Good, direct, honest writing thrives on the active voice.

11. General Advice

This chapter presents general advice on writing. Some advice comes from members of the English Department at the University of Connecticut. Some comes from books on writing. The collection is meant to be eclectic: the writers do not agree on every point. Heed what helps you most. Citations refer to chapter 13, "Short Bibliography of Books on Grammar and Style."

- What is written without effort is in general read without pleasure. (Samuel Johnson)

- **Format:** a clean, well-drafted piece of writing that observes all format conventions. It could serve as a writing sample in a job application. Should be typed or word processed.

  Mechanics: conventions of spelling, punctuation, grammar and syntax are observed; notes and bibliography are included if necessary.

  Structure and Argument: paper has a clear beginning, middle, and end. It has a clear argumentative edge (thesis, point of view) that is sustained by an evocative title, strong opening, and supporting evidence. Transitions between paragraphs are effective.

  Style: paper is fluent and sophisticated. Sentence length varies, and various sentence types (simple, compound, and complex) are employed. Comparisons and analogies (metaphor and simile) are used when appropriate. Diction (word choice) reflects range and precision. Author writes with a real sense of "voice."

Other: paper is enriched by primary and secondary material. Appropriate allusions are invoked as well as class material. (John and Mary Abbott)

- In writing, as in driving a car, you usually look ahead to see where you're going, as well as paying some attention to your current surroundings—with an occasional backward glance to make sure you haven't overlooked something. *So although it's customary to say that you're "following an outline," you're much more likely to be anticipating it.* A scratch outline, in particular, is often a casual guide that will be receptive to adaptation. If your mind races ahead of your pen, jot down fragmentary notes on our outline, on notecards, or [. . .] where they seem to fit. If you can develop them on the spot without getting too distracted, go ahead. But if stopping to expand on each new idea as it occurs to you bogs you down in digressions [. . .] wait to work on the new ideas at the points where they fit into your original design. Anticipation of what's coming will help you to make transitions from one idea to another. It should also help to lead you out of the paragraph you're currently writing and into the next. (Lynn Z. Bloom, *Strategic* 88)

- When you're writing to play with language, for the sake of the sound as much as the literal meaning, you should feel free to take risks. If you want your readers to look at your writing with awe and wonderment, you can ride a galloping syntax across the page with a flamboyant flourish, spurring on those metaphors for all they're worth. But ride goeth before fall; you may want to try a few practice turns in front of the mirror before going out in public in full rodeo regalia. Above all, writing should be fun for you to experiment with. But, as with trick riding, writing is harder to do than it looks; you can learn to do it only through trial and error, and it's potentially dangerous because if you fall, you fall hard. But once you get the hang of it, you can make it look easy, and your readers will admire your bravery as well as your bravura. (Bloom, *Fact* 46)

- One mark of a direct, natural style is that the grammatical sub-jects of the sentences are generally the logical subjects. An-other is that if the sentence conveys an action, the action is found in a verb rather than in a noun.

> **Weak:** His expectation was that a promotion would come from the president of the firm.

Two actions are implied here, expecting and promoting, but both are converted into nouns ("expectation" and "promotion"). The logical subject who is doing the expecting is reduced to the possessive pronoun "His," and the logical subject who is doing the promoting appears as the object of a preposition. The verbs in the sentence, "was" and "would come," are weak and colorless. Presenting the actions as verbs and the agents as subjects produces the following:

> **Better:** He expected that the president of the firm would promote him.

(A. Harris Fairbanks)

- Before there were schools that taught writing and composi-tion, there were writers who studied the best writing they knew and tried to learn the skill of writing by imitation and emulation. A variant of that method involves [. . .] the exami-nation of a variety of writing with an eye to analyzing the tech-niques used in order to acquire more options in writing. Writing is an art, and the path of learning most arts is by ob-serving masters and following some basic instructions. Writ-ing is learned by example and by doing. When you understand the example and realize that most writers' performance is well within your grasp, you can start to learn what you need to know. (Lee A. Jacobus, *Substance* 34)

- Whether the subject matter is a marketing survey, a political issue, or a literary work, writing is a method of communicat-ing information and perceptions. Writing teaches. But before writing becomes an instrument for informing the reader, it serves as a means of learning for the writer. An essay is a pro-cess of discovery as well as a record of what has been discov-ered. One of the chief benefits of writing is that we frequently realize what we want to say only after trying out ideas on a page and seeing our thoughts take shape in language. (Michael Meyer 1)

- The essay exploits the uncertainty of the writer's situation, transforming uncertainty into a fundamental quality of the essay form. [. . .] [T]he essay records the track of an individual mind exploring and resolving a problem. [. . .] [T]he essay must be open to a multiplicity of voices in order to become a means of understanding. (Thomas Recchio)

- Most of the writing you will do in college will have little to do with inspiration or brilliant ideas and much to do with meeting deadlines and assembling data. The key, therefore, is to learn the expected formats for your papers and to develop a sense of how much material you need for a paper of the required length. Basically, most writing is like building bookcases: you want your piece to be clear, orderly, and sturdy. Get a simple design and have plenty of information. Then say what you mean clearly and simply. If inspiration strikes, wonderful: you may produce something brilliant. But even if the Muse avoids you, you will still have a presentable piece of work if your paper is straightforward, well informed, and logical. (Janice Trecker)

- No less than plumbers, cooks, artists, and scuba divers, writers have their tools of the trade. When you settle down to serious composition, have all your gear handy. Have pencils, pens, erasers, paper at your side. Keep your dictionary, grammar book, thesaurus, style manual within reach. Spread out all your notes before you. If the topic of your essay is a text or texts, keep them at hand. For if you do not surround yourself with all your tools, the temptation is great to do without and therefore to fall short of your best. (Martin Veddosso)

- Kill a tree. Be prodigal of paper. Scraps, notes, index cards, outlines, printouts, drafts, edited drafts, redrafts—all stand behind the perfect word, the shapely sentence, the compelling argument. When the essay shines, recycle knowing that the tree did not die in vain. (Morse Tad Vidson)

- If those who have studied the art of writing are in accord on any one point, it is on this: the surest way to arouse and hold the attention of the reader is by being specific, definite, and concrete. The greatest writers—Homer, Dante, Shakespeare—are effective largely because they deal in particulars and report the details that matter. Their words call up pictures. (William Strunk Jr., *Elements* 21)

- Revising is part of writing. Few writers are so expert that they can produce what they are after on the first try. Quite often the writer will discover, on examining the completed work, that there are serious flaws in the arrangement of the material, calling for transpositions. [. . .] Do not be afraid to seize whatever you have written and cut it to ribbons; it can always be restored to its original condition in the morning, if that course seems best. Remember, it is no sign of weakness or defeat that your manuscript ends up in need of major surgery. This as a common occurrence in all writing, and among the best writers. (E. B. White, *Elements* 72)

- [I]magine a football team watching movies of their last game and one of [the players] saying, "I missed a block on that last play; run it again and I'll do it right this time." Impossible! But in writing this is exactly what we do all the time. We run the instant replay and correct our mistakes—not only the mistakes in execution, such as spelling or punctuation, but also the mistakes in conception. That is, if we see that one play isn't working, we can call another play entirely. Think what a tremendous advantage that would give a quarterback. It is an advantage we can all have if we revise and rewrite. If you are the sort of writer who never revises, who never writes a second draft, who thinks of every word as a finished product, you are a prime candidate for writer's block. You may also be doomed to remain at a superficial level of understanding about your subject. To refuse revision is to refuse thought itself. (Robert Scholes, Nancy R. Comley, & Janice Peritz 16)

- Come out with your subject pointed. [. . .] [T]ake a stand. Make a judgment of value, make a *thesis*. Be reasonable, but don't be timid. It is helpful to think of your thesis, your main idea, as a debating question—"Resolved: Welfare payments must go"—taking out the "Resolved" when you actually write the subject down. But your resolution will be even stronger, your essay clearer and tighter, if you can sharpen your thesis

even further—"Resolved: Welfare payments must go be-
cause_____." Fill in that blank, and your worries are practi-
cally over. The main idea is to put your whole argument into
one sentence. (Sheridan Baker, *Practical Stylist* 21)

• The paragraph [. . .] is an integral unit of composition. We can
most easily understand the nature of this unit by comparing it
with the sentence. Like the sentence it has two parts, corresponding to the subject and predicate (understanding the terms
subject and *predicate* in their broad rather than in their narrow
sense). The subject of a paragraph, usually more complicated
than that of a sentence, generally requires a whole sentence for
its full statement [. . .]. The remainder of the paragraph, which
develops or supports that subject, corresponds to the predicate.
[. . .] [H]owever complex they may become, all paragraphs are
really only variations of the subject-predicate pattern, and [. . .]
this pattern is the essence of their structure. (Thomas S. Kane
& Leonard J. Peters, *Practical Rhetoric* 136)

• As natural selection would have it, the human mouth is used in
both eating and speaking. And just as in eating there are rules
of proper etiquette, which tell us how to eat, so in speaking
there are rules of proper usage, which tell us how to speak.
Among the rules for proper eating, two of the most important
are "Use the right fork and don't eat too much." In close correspondence, two of the most important rules for proper speaking are "Use the right word and don't talk too much." (Samuel
R. Levin 1)

• Although we can never free ourselves entirely from the influ-
ences of our own experiences, part of becoming educated is
learning how to stand off somewhat from ourselves and bring
a certain detachment to the subjects we write about. Certainly
it is no part of the definition of the *essay* that it be autobio-
graphical or "familiar," as some writers now call the autobio-
graphical essay. The essence of the essay is that it involves
wrestling by the writer to resolve or clarify an issue. Essays
are, in the current jargon, "think pieces." They involve efforts
to think seriously about important matters. (Richard Marius,
Writer's 40)

- It helps to love words, and a love of words is something that we can develop. The growing writer finds pleasure in becoming a word collector, picking up, examining, and keeping new words (or familiar words seen suddenly, as if for the first time) like seashells or driftwood. Think of the richness in *hogwash* or the exact strength in *rasp*. English abounds in short, strong words. You can collect words from books, of course, but you can also find them in speech; a sense of lively speech adds energy to the best writing. A writer listens to speech—others' and even his own—with a greedy ear. Primitive people and children love words as things in themselves and collect them as ornaments. To become a better writer, rediscover some of the pleasure from words-as-things that you had in your childhood but have probably lost along the way. Patrol the miles of speech looking for words like *flotsam*. (Donald Hall & Sven Birkerts 83-84)

- The Official Style comes in many dialects—government, military, social scientific, lab scientific, MBA flapdoodle—but all exhibit the same basic attributes. They all build on the same central imbalance, a dominance of nouns and an atrophy of verbs. They enshrine the triumph, worshiped in every bureaucracy, of stasis over action. This basic imbalance is easy to cure, if you want to cure it [. . .]. But when do you want to cure it? We all sometimes feel, whatever setting we write in, that we will be penalized for writing in plain English. [. . .] In my academic dialect, that of literary study, writing plain English nowadays is tantamount to walking down the hall naked as a jaybird. (Richard A. Lanham 2)

- (i)   Never use a metaphor, simile, or other figure of speech which you are used to seeing in print.

  (ii)   Never use a long word where a short one will do.

  (iii) If it is possible to cut a word out, always cut it out.

  (iv)   Never use the passive where you can use the active.

    (v)   Never use a foreign phrase, a scientific word, or a jargon word if you can think of an everyday English equivalent.

    (vi)   Break any of these rules sooner than say anything outright barbarous. (George Orwell, "Politics and the English Language)

- There is some justification for a summary at the end of a long paper because the reader may have half forgotten some of the ideas presented thirty pages earlier, but a paper that can easily be held in the mind needs something different. A good concluding paragraph does more than provide an echo of what the writer has already said. It rounds out the previous discussion, normally with a few sentences that summarize (without the obviousness of "We may now summarize"), but it also may draw an inference that has not previously been expressed. To draw such an inference is not to introduce a new idea—a concluding paragraph is hardly the place for a new idea—but is to see the previous material in a fresh perspective. A good concluding paragraph closes the issue while enriching it. (Sylvan Barnet & Marcia Stubbs 76)

- Who casts to write a living line must sweat. (Ben Jonson)

12. Reviewing Your Essay

Twenty-nine distinct damnations
One sure, if another fails
(Robert Browning)

The student with time to revise a composition thoroughly is a figment of the professorial imagination. In reality a teacher can expect papers on which the sweat and tears are still drying.

Nevertheless, a systematic, intelligent revision can improve a paper far more than most writers realize. By and large, the more an author reconsiders a piece of work, the better it will be. So if you can eke out time for review, the essay will almost surely profit.

Two suggestons may help you in revising. First, do not bother to read your work vaguely and passively, waiting for improvements to leap out at you. Instead read over your essay several times, each time with a different, definite aspect of your prose in mind. And second, move from the most general aspects to the most specific and local. Doing so will keep you from wasting time in sprucing up a passage that you later decide to rearrange or omit.

What follows is a list of such aspects for review, arranged in a rough order of narrowing focus. Perhaps only a few scholastic saints or martyrs will reconsider their essay twenty-nine times in twenty-nine different ways. But even the academic rascal would do well to circle especially troublesome items on the list and to review with at least them in mind. After you have finished what you think is a next-to-last draft, read it over repeatedly with one of these questions in mind at a time. Some readings can be very rapid; others must be painstaking.

12.1   **Thesis**. Does the essay have a thesis—one main point? Does the title of the essay indicate the thesis?

12.2   **Train of thought**. Does a train of thought, a developing argument, run throughout the paper? Is this movement of ideas straightforward and evident to a reader? Are there any irrelevant sections?

12.3   **Paragraphing**. Are the paragraphs—the stages of your development—clearly differentiated from one another? Is each paragraph a development of a single idea? Are any paragraphs too long? Are there any irrelevant sentences?

12.4   **Tone**. Is your tone suited to both topic and reader? Is your tone consistent throughout the essay? Are departures from the norm appropriate, justifiable ones?

12.5   **Diction**. Is your level of diction suitable and consistent? Are departures from the norm justifiable?

12.6   **Sentences**. Are all your sentences indeed sentences, or are there fragments or run-ons? Are all your certifiable sentences of readable length, or do some of them go on and on and on and on and?

12.7   **Concision**. Are your sentences free of expansive syntactic constructions and surplus words?

12.8   **Clichés**. Have you avoided clichés and modish terms, which can hinder original thinking? Where you have not, have you freshened them?

12.9   **Imagery**. Are the images embedded in your prose happily mated?

12.10   **Quotations**. Are all quoted passages given correctly? Carefully compare them with the originals.

| 12.11 | **Notation**. Is the source of all quoted passages correctly noted, either in your text or in your notes? |

| 12.12 | **Verbs**. Have you avoided inconsistent shifts in tense throughout your essay? |

| 12.13 | **Pronouns**. Have you avoided inconsistent shifts in person and number throughout your essay? |

| 12.14 | **Reference of pronouns**. Do all your pronouns refer unambiguously to an antecedent word? |

| 12.15 | **Dangling and otherwise disoriented modifiers**. Does each of your introductory modifiers modify the subject of the clause following it? Does each of your other modifiers refer unambiguously to the appropriate word or phrase in the sentence? Can any modifier be relocated closer to its referent without creating awkwardness or ambiguity? |

| 12.16 | **Periods and question marks**. Do all your sentences end with the appropriate punctuation? |

| 12.17 | **Quotation marks**. Are quotation marks used wherever needed? Have you remembered to include the mark at the close of every quotation? Are other marks that are used with quotation marks rightly placed in relation to them? |

| 12.18 | **Commas**. Can you justify your every comma? Have you omitted a comma where one belongs? |

| 12.19 | **Apostrophes**. Have you introduced and rightly placed an apostrophe wherever one is called for? |

| 12.20 | **Other punctuation marks**. Are all other marks properly used? |

| 12.21 | **Numbers**. Have you chosen correctly between numerals and words for your numbers? |

| 12.22 | **Abbreviations**. Are all your abbreviations justifiable? |

| 12.23 | **Capitals**. Are all your capital letters justifiable? Have you failed to capitalize where you should? |

12.24   **Italics**. Are all your italics justifiable? Have you failed to italicize where you should?

12.25   **Spelling**. Have you looked up the spelling of all questionable words? Every last one of them?

At long last you are ready to type your final draft. At least you are almost ready.

12.26   **Format**. Just before you produce the final draft, quickly review the "Format" chapter of the booklet. Do you remember all the details of presentation?

12.27   **Word-division**. Are you properly dividing words run over from one line to the next?

12.28   **Typographical errors**. Have you made any mistakes in transcription? Hunting down such mistakes is important and extremely difficult. See chapter 2 for suggestions on how to proceed.

12.29   **Overview**. Can your essay withstand a close, critical, comprehensive review?

You have now done your best work.

13. Short Bibliography of Books on Grammar and Style

The following list may help you pursue questions of style beyond the confines of this booklet. Some of the books mentioned are basic grammars. Others are more advanced discussions of writing. Still others are directed to special types of prose. The list is short and random, so the absence of a book from the list should not be construed as tacit disapproval of it.

Baker, Sheridan. *The Practical Stylist*. 8th ed. New York: Longman, 1998. Intelligently and engagingly written.

Barnet, Sylvan, and Marcia Stubbs. *Practical Guide to Writing: With Readings*. 7th ed. New York: Harper, 1995. A respected textbook, which takes a rhetorical approach to writing.

Bloom, Lynn Z. *Fact and Artifact: Writing Nonfiction*. 2nd ed. Blair Press Book. Englewood Cliffs, NJ: Prentice, 1994

_____. *Strategic Writing*. New York: Random House, 1983. Bloom is a writer on writing who can write and a prominent scholar in the field.

Boone, Louis E., David L. Kurtz, and Judy R. Block. *Contemporary Business Communication*. 2nd ed. Upper Saddle River, NJ: Prentice, 1997. Recommended for its treatment of business writing.

Chicago Manual of Style. 14th ed. Chicago: U of Chicago P, 1993. Extremely detailed recommendations for "authors, editors, advertisers, typographers, printers, and proofreaders." Has long been the definitive work on style for academic publications.

Cook, Claire Hehrwald. *The MLA's Line by Line: How to Edit Your Own Writing.* Boston: Houghton, 1985.

Crews, Frederick. *The Random House Handbook.* 5th ed. New York: Random, 1987. An intelligently written handbook and rhetoric.

Curme, George O. *English Grammar.* 2nd ed. Barnes and Noble College Outline Series. New York: Harper, 1971. An especially thoroughgoing grammar.

Elbow, Peter. *Writing with Power: Techniques for Mastering the Writing Process.* New York: Oxford UP, 1981.

_____. *Writing without Teachers.* 2nd ed. New York: Oxford UP, 1998. Both books by Elbow are highly regarded by many teachers of writing.

Fowler, H. Ramsey, and Jane E. Aaron. *The Little, Brown Handbook.* 7th ed. New York: Longman, 1998.

Fowler, H. W. *A Dictionary of Modern English Usage.* Ed. Ernest Gowers. 2nd ed. New York: Oxford UP, 1965. Gowers's revision of this celebrated book keeps it the most authoritative, comprehensive, and engaging guide to formal British usage. No bathroom should be without it. There is also a later edition, *Fowler's Modern English Usage.* Ed. R. W. Burchfield. 3d ed. Oxford: Clarendon, 1996. This edition is more descriptive, less prescriptive than either of the earlier ones.

Gibaldi, Joseph. *MLA Handbook for Writers of Research Papers.* 4th ed. New York: MLA, 1995. Detailed and authoritative.

_____. *MLA Style Manual and Guide to Scholarly Publishing.* 2nd ed. New York: MLA, 1998. Even more detailed than the *MLA Handbook*.   Treats at length documenting electronic publications.

Gibson, Walker. *Tough, Sweet & Stuffy*. Bloomington: Indiana UP, 1966. A personable account of how a writer sounds on the page.

Hacker, Diana. *Rules for Writers: A Brief Handbook*. 3d ed. Boston: Bedford, 1996.

Hall, Donald, and Sven Birkerts. *Writing Well*. 9th ed. New York: Longman, 1998.   A well-written book, which teaches by example as well as precept. Both authors are professional writers and conscientious teachers of writing.

Heffernan, James A., and John E. Lincoln. *Writing: A College Handbook*.   4th ed.   New York: Norton, 1994.   A comprehensive   textbook,   which   treats   procedural, rhetorical, and grammatical aspects of writing.

Hodges, John C., et al. *Hodges' Harbrace College Handbook*. 13th ed. New York: Harcourt, 1998. A standard, popular handbook of grammar.

Jacobus, Lee A. *Substance, Style, and Strategy*. New York: Oxford UP, 1998. A comprehensive guide for students in advanced composition courses.

Kane, Thomas S. *The Oxford Guide to Writing*. New York: Oxford UP, 1983. A sane, comprehensive text on writing. Especially rich in examples.

Lambuth, David. *The Golden Book on Writing*. New York: Viking, 1964. A brief, witty treatment of language and style.

Lanham, Richard A. *Revising Prose*. 3d ed. New York: Macmillan, 1992. Perceptive advice on revision.

Lee, Mary, et al. *Handbook of Technical Writing: Form and Style*. New York: Harcourt, 1990. Recommended for its treatment of technical writing.

Levin, Samuel R. *Shades of Meaning: Reflections on the Use, Misuse, and Abuse of English*. Boulder, CO: Westview, 1998. Heavy, testy, and moralistic, even by my standards, but good on wrestling with shades of meaning.

Kramer, Melinda G., Glenn C. Leggett, and David Mead. *Prentice-Hall Handbook for Writers*. 12th ed. Englewood Cliffs, NJ: Prentice, 1995. A standard, popular handbook of grammar.

Marius, Richard. *A Writer's Companion*. 3d ed. New York: McGraw, 1995. Written by a successful writer and dedicated teacher.

Marius, Richard, and Harvey S. Wiener. *The McGraw-Hill College Handbook*. 2nd ed. New York: McGraw, 1988. An ambitious academic handbook. Includes good advice on writing with a computer.

Meyer, Michael. *The Little, Brown Guide to Writing Research Papers*. 3d ed. Boston: Little, 1994. Readable, reliable advice for every stage, from beginning the research to polishing the paper.

Sale, Roger. *On Writing*. New York: Random, 1970. An intelligent essay on writing.

Schiffhorst, Gerald J., and Donald Pharr. *The Short Handbook for Writers*. 2nd ed. New York: McGraw, 1997.

Scholes, Robert, Nancy R. Comley, and Janice Peritz. *The Practice of Writing*. 4th ed. New York: St. Martin's, 1994. A rhetoric book written with verve. Exercises include describing a Rube Goldberg cartoon and comparing the smile of Mona Lisa with that of Bart Simpson.

Silverman, Jay, Elaine Hughes, and Diana Roberts Wienbroer. *Rules of Thumb: A Guide for Writers*. 3d ed. New York: McGraw, 1996. Helpful, easily remembered advice.

Strunk, William Jr., and E. B. White. *The Elements of Style*. 3d ed. New York: Macmillan, 1979. An all-too-short, enjoyable guidebook, in which White's urbanity sweetens (and undermines) Strunk's rectitude.

Williams, Joseph M. *Style: Ten Lessons in Clarity and Grace*. 5th ed. New York: Longman, 1997. Thoughtful, sensible considerations on writing standard English.